LEADERSHIP
MEDITATIONS

Reflections for Leaders in All Walks of Life

Edited and selected by David Goetz
and the editors of Christianity Today International

TYNDALE HOUSE PUBLISHERS, INC.
WHEATON, ILLINOIS

Visit Tyndale's exciting Web site at www.tyndale.com

Leadership Meditations: Reflections for Leaders in All Walks of Life

This book was developed by Leadership Resources of Christianity Today International.

Designed by Melinda Schumacher

Edited by Susan Taylor

Library of Congress Cataloging-in-Publication Data

Printed in the United States of America

07	06	05	04	03	02	01
7	6	5	4	3	2	1

⮌CONTENTS

⌒INTRODUCTION

It's easy for us to feel overwhelmed by the fact that God has called us to lead. That he has entrusted to us the responsibility of caring for other people, guiding an organization, solving problems, pointing the way for our families or others under our influence. King David, too, must have felt overwhelmed when he considered God's call on his life.

When Psalm 78 lists "the praiseworthy deeds of the Lord, his power, and the wonders he has done" (NIV), it includes God's parting the Red Sea, guiding the Israelites by a supernatural fire, making water gush from a rock, and dropping a flaky, delicious white food out of the sky. But the psalm concludes with a deed that should astound anyone: "He [God] chose David his servant and took him from the sheep pens; from tending the sheep he brought him to be the shepherd of his people Jacob, of Israel his inheritance. And David shepherded them with integrity of heart; with skillful hands he led them" (vv. 70-71).

It's a miracle that God would choose a kid who didn't know much except how to take care of farm animals. It's a marvel that God would entrust his people to David's care. It's a wonder that God would transfer David from a pen to a palace (by way of a cave). No wonder David prayed, "Who am I, O Lord God, and what is my family, that you have brought me this far? . . . You speak as though I were someone very great, O Lord God" (1 Chron. 17:16-17).

When we feel overwhelmed by the responsibilities of

leadership, all we can do, in our mixture of fear and gratitude, is what David did: try to live up to the honor and the weight and the responsibility.

This book offers fifty-two meditations to help Christian leaders—not just pastors and teachers but those who exercise leadership in business, education, medicine, home and family, and other arenas—become more Christlike in their role as leaders. Written by Christian leaders from a variety of backgrounds and compiled by the editors of *Leadership* journal, the meditations will help you to grow in your relationships with those over whom you have a position of leadership.

How can you get the most out of this book?

The book is arranged topically; that is, each of the fifty-two meditations relates to a particular theme. Of course, you may choose to read through the book in order, one meditation at a time; you might even decide to read one meditation each week for a year. But you can also use the **topical index** in the back of the book to help you locate meditations that relate to a specific challenge you are facing in your role as a leader. The meditations in this book focus on external aspects of leadership—on the outward actions of effective Christian leaders. For example, the leader of a board of deacons could choose a meditation that deals with an issue the board is facing—perhaps servanthood or outreach—and use it to open a deacons meeting. A parent or business professional might choose a meditation related to family or conflict that applies to an issue in the home or workplace. The index lists each meditation under both a primary topic (the theme that is indicated at the beginning of each meditation) and several secondary topics, giving the greatest possible applicability to each meditation. We've also included a **Scripture index** to enable readers to locate meditations that are based on a specific portion of Scripture.

All of us are leaders in one way or another. Whether you have the opportunity to influence the lives of those in your family, your church, your neighborhood, or your workplace, this book can help you to be a more effective leader in the place where God has put you. Psalm 78 says that David led with integrity and skill. May this book help you in your quest to do the same.

Kevin A. Miller
Vice President
Christianity Today International

BALANCE

The Right Size

We are telling you about what we ourselves have actually seen and heard, so that you may have fellowship with us. And our fellowship is with the Father and with his Son, Jesus Christ. We are writing these things so that our joy will be complete.

1 JOHN 1:3-4

HOW often do we find ourselves searching for just the right size in something we want or need? When we try on shoes or a shirt, we look for the right size, but the issue applies to other areas of our lives as well. How many people can I really know well? How many projects and jobs can I accomplish before I approach burnout? Questions of time and money management crop up: How much time should I spend at work, at play, on the Internet? How much money do I need to earn to be a responsible provider and yet a wise and generous steward? We wonder about the size of a group: What is the right size for a city? a school? a church? a family?

As I see it, the answer to all of these questions goes beyond mere numbers. Some families of three have more interpersonal fellowship than families of six; and some families of six notice and celebrate the uniqueness of each child more than families with only one child. There are single-parent families that have become the right size because faith, hope, and love have filled the empty place left by the missing parent.

We are the answer to the questions about size—if we care enough to take the place that only we can fill and then in friendliness reach out to the person on each side. When we do that, even the largest and most complicated gathering of people will be just the right size.

Size is like time; it comes down to a question of equilibrium and rhythm so that the answer lies in learning to balance large and small, fast and slow, many and few.

Any size is right when we do the work it takes to know someone else by name and when someone knows our name. Then our families and our churches are just the right size.

—Earl Palmer

REFLECTION

Have I found the right size for my church? my family? my fellowship? my circle of obligation?

PRAYER

Lord, thank you for including me in your forever family. I am grateful that you have invited men and women, girls and boys of all ages and races into the fellowship that shares the love and faithfulness of Jesus Christ our Lord.

"The Bible is all about community: from the Garden of Eden to the City at the end."

—George F. MacLeod, Presbyterian minister

And about reconciliation — God always drawing us back to himself — until that day when we will live up them in the forever City of God.

CALLING

Too Old to Hear the Voice of God?

The boy Samuel was serving the
Lord by assisting Eli. Now in
those days messages from the Lord
were very rare, and visions were
quite uncommon. . .

*   Suddenly, the Lord called out,*
"Samuel! Samuel!"

*   "Yes?" Samuel replied. "What*
is it?"

1 SAMUEL 3:1, 4

FOR as long as I can remember, when I heard the story of God's calling little Samuel while he lived with the old priest Eli, I had always identified with Samuel. While I was still much too young to understand the full implications, God had called me to serve him as a leader in his church. Similarly, Samuel's story is about God calling a boy, a boy far too young to understand the full meaning of that call at the time.

But then one day I realized that I was starting to identify with Eli. He had been working in the temple for a lifetime. Had God ever awakened him in the middle of the night, calling him by his very own name? Why had God spoken only to this Samuel, a boarder in the Lord's house, but not to old, experienced, dedicated Eli?

Here I am, having served the Lord as a pastor for over thirty years. Some little upstart in his early twenties shows up, telling me that God has spoken to him. Why has God not spoken directly to me? Why does he insist on speaking to someone half my years?

Here is my church, shrinking in membership. On the edge of town is that new, young church. Their building is not nearly as nice as ours. They obviously have a less-able and less-experienced pastor! Why does God bless their efforts so profusely?

The account of young Samuel and old Eli becomes a story for those of us in the latter stages of our careers. To serve God means to let God be God—sovereign. He is free to bypass us and go to those young upstarts who do not have our maturity, experience, and wisdom. In each generation God calls those whom he calls.

Why does God do this? Maybe he does it to keep proving to us that the church is of God, not of us. God keeps sustaining the church by infusing new life into it—by calling people whom we might not have called.

One of my mentors was Carlyle Marney, a great Baptist prophet of the South. I first met him when I was in college. Then I ran into him again just after I was out of seminary. I was talking to Marney about an experience in which God's presence and grace seemed particularly real to me.

Marney listened thoughtfully, and then I asked him, "Are you surprised that God might reveal something like this?"

"No," Marney replied. "What surprises me is that God revealed something that wonderful to a kid like you and not to me!"

Is the calling of Samuel a good-news story or a bad-news story? Your take on it may have something to do with how long you have been at this business of Christian vocation.

—William Willimon

REFLECTION

Do I encourage younger, emerging leaders? Do I respect and seek out those with more wisdom and experience?

PRAYER

Sovereign God, in every generation you choose to call certain people—whether we like it or not. Yet you reveal yourself to all who call upon you. Whether we actually hear your voice or not, keep us open to your presence and mindful of your purpose for us.

"The error of youth is to believe that intelligence is a substitute for experience, while the error of age is to believe that experience is a substitute for intelligence."

—Lyman Bryson (1888–1959), American educator

8

CALLING

How Do You Want to Be Remembered?

*Choose a good reputation over
great riches, for being held in high
esteem is better than having silver
or gold.*

PROVERBS 22:1

NEVER before in history have people had the opportunity to have a second adulthood. At the turn of the century, life expectancy was fifty years. Now people live an average of at least thirty years past that, and we are more affluent than previous generations. We are pioneers on a new demographic frontier full of new opportunities. In fact, the second half of life is or can be better than the first half.

While statistically we may live longer, we still don't know exactly when we will die. But all of us, if we wish, may select our own epitaphs. I have chosen mine. It is a fairly haunting thing to think about your gravestone while you are alive. Yet my epitaph stands as both a glorious inspiration and an epic challenge. Adapted from the parable of the sower in Matthew 13, it reads: "100x means 100 times."

You may call my 100x epitaph wishful thinking. But when you select an epitaph as an expression of gratitude, you identify yourself as someone with a purpose and a passion. I'm an entrepreneur, and I want to be remembered as being good soil where the seed multiplied a hundredfold. It is how I wish and attempt to live; it expresses my passions and my core commitments; and it is how

I envision my legacy. I want to be a symbol of higher yield, in both life and in death.

Take the opportunity to write your own epitaph. Where is God calling you to serve? What passion has he instilled in your heart? Each of us has been given something to work with—time, money, and/or ideas. Using all of who you are in service to God and to people in your community will lead to a deeper, more fulfilling sense of accomplishment.

—Bob Buford

11

REFLECTION

What would I like my legacy to be?

PRAYER

Lord, give me a spirit of expectancy as I await the adventures you may have for me in the years to come!

"He who has influence upon the heart of God rules the world."

—Helmut Thielicke (1908–1985), German Protestant theologian

12

CALLING

Talking Billboards

*In the sixth month of Elizabeth's
pregnancy, God sent the angel
Gabriel to Nazareth, a village in
Galilee, to a virgin named Mary.
She was engaged to be married to
a man named Joseph, a
descendant of King David.
Gabriel appeared to her and said,
"Greetings, favored woman! The
Lord is with you!"*

LUKE 1:26-28

HE burst into my office one afternoon exclaiming, "I've at last found out what God wants me to do with my life!"

Having logged many hours with him as he pondered what to do after graduation, I was certainly interested that he had come to such a sure conviction of what God wanted him to do.

"It was clear as day. I was driving to my job and was stuck in traffic for a few minutes," he said. "There was this billboard over to the left, with a bush growing in front of it. All you could see were the letters *G-O*. 'Go.' I drove on for another few minutes, and traffic stopped again. The pickup truck in front of me had a bumper sticker on the back of it, but it was partly torn off. All that was left were the letters *N-O-W*. Get it? 'Go now.' Of course I knew what I should do. I'm going into elementary school teaching and not to law school."

I sat there stunned, thinking, *And this is a soon-to-be college graduate?* Aloud I said, "Look, that's a bush in front of a billboard and a torn bumper sticker. Why would you think that would be the voice of God?"

Crestfallen, he said, "Well, I guess you would have to have been there to get it. But it was clear as day."

We are taught, as modern people, that we live in a closed universe. There is no word other than that word that arises from within us. We are the captains of our fate, the masters of our souls. What we ought to do in life is a matter of our deciding what we ought to do.

Scripture beckons us toward a more open, complicated, and interesting world, a world where women like Mary received messages from God, a world where our lives are capable of being disrupted, jerked around, intruded upon, by a voice that is not self-derived.

I heard the distinguished Old Testament scholar Walter Brueggemann say, "It is a sad thing to live an uncalled life. We have a whole generation who has nothing more to do with their lives than what they decide. Vocation is a great blessing."

And it is. To be able to live one's life for something more important than oneself, to have one's life grasped, grabbed, commanded for some good larger than one's own desires, this is great good news.

Our lives are not our own. We are not left to our own devices. We are called. Thank God.

—William Willimon

REFLECTION

Am I engaged in those spiritual disciplines that can help my spirit to be attentive to God's leading?

PRAYER

Holy God, there are so many "signs" that might be from you—or might not. Grant us the discernment to separate the imagined from the real, and the wisdom to test everything according to your revealed Word.

"The great thing is to get the true picture, whatever it is."

—Winston Churchill (1874–1965),
British statesman

CHALLENGE

Lord, I Can't Do This!

*Forgetting the past and looking
forward to what lies ahead, I
strain to reach the end of the race
and receive the prize for which
God, through Christ Jesus, is
calling us up to heaven.*

PHILIPPIANS 3:13-14

WHEN I tried out for the cheerleading squad in seventh grade, there were only two openings. Every girl knew that Susie, the most coordinated, popular, and enthusiastic of us all, was guaranteed a position. The only question was who would earn the second spot. For weeks we practiced our moves to two assigned cheers and jumped the three protocol jumps.

On tryout day we were given numbers to objectify the process, and we waited in line, watching the girls who auditioned before us. Laura did better than her knobby knees usually allowed. Linda's athleticism was perfect, but her voice too quiet. Kathy's whole performance was solid. Then it was Susie's turn. We were all ready to watch her strut her stuff.

"Go back! Go back!" she chanted. "Go back into the woods because you haven't got, haven't got, you haven't got the goods."

The words were right, but the motions were wrong; they were the moves from the other cheer. It was a moment of group anxiety as we tried to silently signal Susie of her mistake, but her face told us she already knew. Everyone in the room was silently crying, *Let her try again.* But the head judge thanked her and asked for the next candidate.

Because of Susie's blunder, my name was one of the two announced the next Monday morning. I was suddenly propelled to a task I had not truly envisioned myself having. I asked myself, *Will I be able to do this? Why did they pick me?* Through the first three practices I was embarrassed and kept blushing. Feeling singled out and unsure of myself in my new role, my prayer was simply, *Oh, God, help me!*

That was not the last time I felt ill-prepared to bear the responsibilities of a new position. New professional roles, including complex tasks of management and leadership, have placed new demands on me in recent years. I often need to shift and balance those that are heavy and difficult, shouldering them for the long haul. But God's guiding strength leads me step-by-step, away from negative assumptions of the past and toward a confidence rooted in his care.

—Mary C. Miller

19

REFLECTION

When faced with a challenging task, how do I respond? How does God want me to respond?

PRAYER

God—alone I can't. But with you and through you and for you, I can. Let me always rest in that assurance.

"We have given too much attention to methods and to machinery and to resources, and too little to the Source of Power, the filling with the Holy Ghost."

—J. Hudson Taylor, nineteenth-century missionary to China

6

CHALLENGE

No Easy Work

*Then I heard the Lord asking,
"Whom should I send as a
messenger to my people? Who will
go for us?"*

*And I said, "Lord, I'll go! Send
me."*

ISAIAH 6:8

IN the church sometimes we'll call up somebody in mid-August and say, "Sorry we're late, but we wonder if you would like to teach the eighth-grade Sunday school class starting right after Labor Day. It doesn't take much preparation. It's not a lot of hard work. You can do it. We know you can."

That's no way to get anybody to reach his or her potential. It's wrong to offer people easy work. Few things in life are more insulting than to be offered an easy job.

Many years ago my wife and I attended a church that was having some special problems with a high school class. These kids were tough to handle. So they asked a capable, experienced woman in the church to help.

"Mary," they said, "we'd like you to take this class. They're unmanageable, and we don't know what can be done with them."

They challenged her in a wonderful way.

—Max De Pree

23

REFLECTION

What challenging work is Jesus calling me to this week?

PRAYER

Lord, help me to honor those I lead by giving them work that challenges them to grow.

"The job of a football coach is to make men do what they don't want to do, in order to achieve what they've always wanted to be."

—Tom Landry, late professional football coach

COMMUNITY

United in Suffering

*All praise to the God and Father
of our Lord Jesus Christ. He is the
source of every mercy and the God
who comforts us. He comforts us
in all our troubles so that we can
comfort others. When others are
troubled, we will be able to give
them the same comfort God has
given us.*

2 CORINTHIANS 1:3-4

I'VE always wondered what makes community biblical—as opposed to community that is merely social. So often churches provide merely social community (often called fellowship), which meets a genuine need for friendships and a place where, as the old *Cheers* theme burned into our minds, "everyone knows your name." But recently I experienced for the first time a more profound sense of biblical community.

For the past seven years my wife and I have participated in a small group that today is composed of five couples. This past year our group celebrated the birth of one child. We also cheered raucously when two other women in the group got pregnant, and then we prayed fervently for safe deliveries and healthy babies. Both women were due within weeks of each other. In October the woman who was due first became concerned when her due date came and went. She said the baby seemed to be moving less. But the ultrasound detected a strong heartbeat on Monday. On Tuesday there was no heartbeat. On Wednesday morning she gave birth to Ian Patrick, whom we would never get to know. The umbilical cord was wrapped twice around his neck.

My wife and I—and several others from our small group—were at the hospital Wednesday morning when Ian was born. First his grandpa came out to the waiting room, followed by his dad, and then the doctor. We huddled together sobbing, staring down at our shoes. We attempted to pray. Then we all went to the delivery room to see Ian's mom and Ian's body.

The week dragged by. After the funeral we collapsed from exhaustion. As I grieved with the parents and the other members of my small group, I gained a fresh insight on biblical community: Some spiritual growth can happen only through suffering. But in this life, suffering is not evenly meted out. Especially in the suburbs, where people tend to keep their suffering private, one can go for long stretches without smelling the stench of death.

Community forced me into relationship with a small circle of people who are becoming closer than family. I was forced to suffer loss—albeit vicariously but real nonetheless. Community is not just a place for those who are suffering to find comfort but for those who are comfortable to find suffering. Together we join Christ in his suffering, and as a result, "When others are troubled, we [are] able to give them the same comfort God has given us" (2 Cor. 1:4).

—David Goetz

27

REFLECTION

Where can I become more connected with other Christians so that I might weep with those who weep and rejoice with those who rejoice?

PRAYER

Lord, being in biblical community demands all of me; give me the courage and grace to give myself to my brothers and sisters in Christ.

"What happens when God grants the gift of genuine Christian fellowship? Deep, joyful sharing replaces the polite prattle typically exchanged by Christians on Sunday mornings."

—Ronald Sider, author and advocate
for social justice

CONFESSION

The Lie of Loneliness

*But now, O Israel, the Lord who
created you says: "Do not be
afraid, for I have ransomed you. I
have called you by name; you are
mine.*

ISAIAH 43:1

IN April 1995 we experienced a student revival on our campus that dramatically illustrated the power of feeling known by God. Students in a chapel service spontaneously began to confess their sins in public. Streaming up to the microphone, they spoke openly of their sins and struggles. Short of murder, I can't think of a sin that wasn't confessed or a struggle that wasn't shared. Rape, incest, drug abuse, eating disorders—all were aired in front of hundreds of people. Each student would speak, walk away from the microphone, and be surrounded by friends. Hugs, tears, and prayers of encouragement and healing followed. This went on for several nights.

Throughout their lives these young people had been told a lie, a lie that said, "You're alone in your struggles. No one knows you." That's a terrible feeling to live with. They longed to be known—don't we all? But at the same time, it's terrifying to lay oneself bare before others.

The Spirit moved among those students to give them the gift of being known. He empowered them to discover, finally, that to be completely transparent and to feel completely loved is to come closer to the heart of God. So it is for all of us. The gift of prayer is that we can lay all that we are before God, who won't be surprised or shocked at anything we say.

—Ben Patterson

REFLECTION

Is there anyone alongside before whom I can "lay myself bare" in prayer?

PRAYER

God, thank you for creating and bringing other people to us to help us bear our burdens.

"You never find yourself until you face the truth."

—Pearl Bailey, twentieth-century
American entertainer

9

CONFLICT

The Enemy Next Door

*You have heard that the law of
Moses says, "Love your neighbor"
and hate your enemy. But I say,
love your enemies! Pray for those
who persecute you!*
MATTHEW 5:43-44

WHEN a windstorm collapsed the fence between our yard and our neighbor's, he proposed that each of us charge our respective insurance companies the full amount, which was not only unethical but illegal. Upon repairing the fence, he gave me a bill, assuming I had received full payment for the fence rather than the half I had submitted a claim for. I ignored his bill and gave him his rightful share. He was angry, but I didn't realize it until the next time it snowed.

Since he had the only snowblower on the block, upon completing his walk, he usually did ours and that of the widow who lived on the other side of us. This time, however, he did his walk, took the snowblower into the street to avoid our walk, and then took care of the widow's sidewalk. I could see the evidence of his anger in our snow-covered walk and the clear path he had made in the street.

My relationship with my neighbor was parallel to David's relationship with King Saul. David did not wrong Saul, but Saul became his enemy, even trying to kill David on many occasions. In 1 Samuel 26, Saul and David meet; only this time David seeks out Saul, finding him and all of his men asleep. He goes into Saul's camp and in the process keeps Abishai from killing Saul. The next morning David awakens the king and tells him that he had protected Saul better than Saul's own bodyguards. David learned that God expected him to seek out his adversaries and serve them righteously.

I knew that if I was going to ask people to follow David's example, I had to do likewise. It took a while, but two months after the sidewalk incident I sat down and wrote a letter to my neighbor. I apologized for offending him and, going the extra mile, enclosed a check for the full amount. I also told him that my relationship to Jesus Christ motivated me to act in this way, and I asked him to consider a similar relationship.

He never said a word to me. But that summer the widow next door told me that he just could not get over the letter I had sent him. She said, "I don't know what you told him, but it made a significant impact."

My neighbor is not yet a believer, and I am still praying for him. But the experience taught me that if I am to serve as God desires, I must treat my enemy with fairness, forbearance, and forgiveness—even if that "enemy" lives next door.

—Paul Borden

REFLECTION

How do I treat people I don't particularly like?

PRAYER

Father, I find it hard to deal with _____.
Help me to treat this person as Jesus would.

"The wonder of forgiveness has become a banality. It can be the death of our faith if we forget that it is literally a miracle."

—Helmut Thielicke (1908–1985),
German Protestant theologian

36

10

DEATH

Better Than Optimism

*For we know that when this
earthly tent we live in is taken
down—when we die and leave
these bodies—we will have a
home in heaven, an eternal body
made for us by God himself and
not by human hands. . . . So we
are always confident, even though
we know that as long as we live in
these bodies we are not at home
with the Lord.*

2 CORINTHIANS 5:1, 6

OUR oldest daughter died a few years ago. The Bible tells us to rejoice always. How do you rejoice under those circumstances?

Although my wife and I are still weeping, we can rejoice in our total assurance that we know where our daughter is and that we loved her and provided her the best medical care available. Psalm 139:16 says God set her death date from the foundation of the earth. In weeping we can still have joy, but joy is a condition you're in because of a decision you made.

In times of weeping, joy is the only thing in life worth having. Our daughter's death is the most difficult thing I've experienced, and yet I've felt God's presence so strongly since then. It has brought me closer to the Lord than anything since my salvation.

About a month after the funeral my wife and I were in Washington, D.C. On Saturday morning as we headed for the elevator to go to breakfast, I thought, *I wonder what Susie's doing right now?* And then just as quickly another thought hit me: *I know exactly where she is. I know exactly what she's doing.*

Every parent always wants to know where his or her children are, regardless of their age. I didn't have a clue where my other kids were, but I knew where Susie was. The joy in knowing she was fine—better than fine—was overwhelming.

I'm a born optimist; I'll take my last two dollars and buy a money belt with it. But there's a big difference between the joy of optimism and the joy that comes with knowing you're in God's will, that he has already won this deal. All I've got to do is collect. It's not what I do; it's what Christ did.

—Zig Ziglar

I have said this all along - There is
joy even in great sorrow

Depression does't preclude
- I have hope

Get help (med) for the
clinical → Dr/ Therapist / meds
Get help (the) for spiritual →
Christ / Holy Spirit God the Father

REFLECTION

How much of my life do I live with an eye on eternity?

PRAYER

The reality of heaven—help me to know it, Lord.
Know it as sure as I know the chair I'm sitting in.
Know it both for myself and for my loved ones
who already live with you there.

*"We see heaven more clearly through the prism of
tears."*

> —Robertson McQuilkin, author and
> retired college president

40

*Each day /
Each moment
an eye towards heaven*

11

DECISION MAKING

Questions for Better Decisions

Afterward Paul felt impelled by the Holy Spirit to go over to Macedonia and Achaia before returning to Jerusalem. "And after that," he said, "I must go on to Rome!" . . . He was preparing to sail back to Syria when he discovered a plot by some Jews against his life, so he decided to return through Macedonia. . . . Paul had decided against stopping at Ephesus this time because he didn't want to spend further time in the province of Asia. He was hurrying to get to Jerusalem, if possible, for the Festival of Pentecost.

ACTS 19:21; 20:3, 16

MANY Christian leaders are handicapped because they almost inevitably think only in moralistic terms: right versus wrong. "What's the *right* thing to do? What *ought* to be done?"

But there are other modes to consider: effective versus ineffective, good versus best, safe versus risky. Virtually every decision has a moral aspect, either in its consequences or in the way the decision will be implemented. And most of us in the ministry carry an intuitive desire to reach for the godly, to hear the words of God on a given issue and line up with him rather than against him. But not all church administration deals with Mount Sinai issues. Many decisions are more mundane and subtle.

A leader needs to be asking: What are my options? Who should be involved in the decision-making process? How do I know when I have enough information? When is it time to bite the bullet and decide?

These are questions we don't ask often enough.

—Carl F. George

REFLECTION

What decisions that I am facing need more thought?

PRAYER

Lord, give me discernment. Help me distinguish between decisions in which the most important factor is moral and those in which strategy is the key.

"The best decision-makers are those who are willing to suffer the most over their decisions but still retain their ability to be decisive."

—M. Scott Peck, psychiatrist and author

44

12

EVANGELISM

No Charter for Comfort

*Don't be selfish; don't live to
make a good impression on others.
Be humble, thinking of others as
better than yourself. Don't think
only about your own affairs, but
be interested in others, too, and
what they are doing.*

PHILIPPIANS 2:3-4

I S there anything simpler or more natural than members of a church looking out for their own interests? We like to park conveniently. We want our pew available each week. We expect our kind of music to be sung—not that other ungodly stuff! We like things our way, to our convenience and our taste. How easy it is to make church nice and comfortable—for us.

Yet the church isn't meant to be comfortable. No pioneering, radical, countercultural organization has the leisure of being comfortable. A country club can be comfortable. A golfing foursome can be comfortable. A family gathering can be comfortable. But a church—that culture-shaking, eternity-changing band Jesus commissioned to turn the world upside down—doesn't have the charter to be comfortable. It's commissioned as an activist for the kingdom of God!

My pleasure, my ease, my way—such things are really not important. God's glory, God's tasks, others' benefit—those are the reasons for the church's existence. The apostle Paul says we are to treat others as more important than ourselves. We are to be "put out" by the interests of others. The church is not my personal vending machine. Instead, it is a lifesaving station for reaching out to those in peril needing to be made safe.

How does that happen? It happens when leaders decide that their responsibility is to follow seriously the One who came to seek and to save the lost.

That, however, gets expensive when the church has to add parking and pews and programs for those not yet in the church. That becomes difficult when the comfortable become discomfited by change. That becomes messy when the sacred mixes with the profane. Granted.

Yet Jesus emptied himself, humbled himself, and died on a cross for us—and that is to be our mind-set (Phil. 2:5-11). As leaders we must proclaim to the comfortable the message of Christ and then refocus our thinking and strategy on the outsider, so that every tongue may confess that Jesus Christ is Lord.

—James D. Berkley

47

REFLECTION

In what areas am I expecting the church to meet my needs? Are any of these areas impinging on the church's ability to reach out?

PRAYER

Discomfort me, Lord, when I want to get comfortable, and help me to use my church not merely as my personal religious social club but as a rescue station for those who desperately need you.

"The church is not a museum for finished products. It's a hospital for the sick."

—Bruce Larson, writer

48

13

EVANGELISM

Not off the Hook

How can they call on him to save them unless they believe in him? And how can they believe in him if they have never heard about him? And how can they hear about him unless someone tells them? And how will anyone go and tell them without being sent? That is what the Scriptures mean when they say, "How beautiful are the feet of those who bring good news!"

ROMANS 10:14-15

SOMETIMES in evangelism we try to assume the Holy Spirit's role, but the much greater problem is our hoping the Holy Spirit will do our job for us. One popular version of evangelism says, "If I just live as a consistent Christian, people will see it, figure it out, and come to Christ." But that approach isn't biblical, and it doesn't work. In Romans 10:14 Paul said we have to go and give people the message. We have to initiate conversations and trust the Holy Spirit will work as we bring the message to those we converse with.

Another temptation is to ride on the positive experience people have when they come to a church program; we imagine they will be interested enough in what they've seen to figure it all out on their own.

Years ago a girl I knew from high school started coming to a Bible study I was leading. She learned the songs and started talking like us and hanging out with us. One day I said to her, "I'm glad you're part of our group."

"I love it," she replied.

"I'm just wondering," I said, "have you ever come to the point of committing your life to Christ so you know your sins are forgiven?"

"No, I've never done that," she said, "and no one ever told me I needed to." I learned we have to keep spelling out the basics.

—Mark Mittelberg

51

REFLECTION

Who among my friends and colleagues might be open to the things of God?

PRAYER

Lord, I don't ever want to take for granted my role in helping others come to you. Help me to do what I'm called to do in each relationship, both as a model of your love and as a communicator of your gospel.

"Consumer relationship development is as important as product development."

—Frank P. Perdue, founder of the giant poultry business

14

FAMILY

Cardboard Daddy

*Your wife will be like a fruitful
vine, flourishing within your
home. And look at all those
children! There they sit around
your table as vigorous and healthy
as young olive trees.*
PSALM 128:3

ARLIER this year an article floated into my electronic in-box from the Ziff-Davis Network. It heralded yet another computer breakthrough from a major corporation.

Sidi Yomtov, an Israeli chip designer working for National Semiconductor, developed a way to combine 43 different PC chips onto a single silicon wafer—miniaturization that makes big news in the ever-shrinking world of personal computers. The author described the pressure National Semiconductor experienced and, by extension, the stress Mr. Yomtov felt as the lead designer of the new chip:

> Coordinating a team of 90 engineers in four different time zones, [Yomtov] is at work or on the road so much that his three daughters in Tel Aviv erected a life-size cardboard cut-out of him in the family's living room. "I put my entire prestige of two decades at National behind this project," says the bleary-eyed Yomtov. "I was afraid that if it didn't work, I might not be able to show my face. . . ."
>
> Yomtov, meanwhile, expects the next version of his chip to be ready in six months.

As I read that, I wondered if the cardboard cutout was a family joke or a Band-Aid over a festering wound. *How sad,* I thought, *that a man could be so worried about losing face that he risks losing his family.*

And then I felt the Lord challenge me: How many times have I placed my career before my wife, my family, and my own spiritual well-being? How many times have I stayed late in the office to write one more e-mail or finish one more task? How many times have I allowed the pursuit of recognition among my peers to overshadow the needs of my family? How often have I gone home only to obsess over unfinished office work, wandering through the weekend distracted and dimensionless, not sharing myself with my family?

I have resolved to take stock regularly of my life: Is my involvement at home three-dimensional or only a two-dimensional cardboard proxy? My family needs me—not a substitute, a Kodak memory, or the mere promise (or threat) of my presence. As I complete that thought, now is a good time to leave the office and enjoy an evening with my wife.

—Rich Tatum

55

REFLECTION

Why is it often easier to pour myself into my work than into my family?

PRAYER

Father, give me the strength to serve my family with my whole being.

"Married life offers no panacea—if it is going to reach its potential, it will require an all-out investment by both husband and wife."

—James C. Dobson, psychologist and author

56

FAMILY

Dinner Companions

*A bowl of soup with someone you
love is better than steak with
someone you hate.*
PROVERBS 15:17

THIS past week was rough. Last night I attended a banquet honoring the young people who will confirm their baptismal vows and become adult members of the congregation. The previous night I had a late afternoon visitation and an early evening funeral followed by dinner. The night before that, the executive committee held its monthly meeting over pizza. I was home for dinner the night before that, but the previous four days, I was out of town at a seminary board meeting.

Spending only one evening out of eight with my family made my week horrible. I could justify not spending time with my family by claiming I was doing the Lord's work or by asserting that my children don't need me around as much since they're grown up.

Yet while my family may get along without me, I can't get along without them. When I haven't had the chance to sit down at the table with the people who know me best and love me most, I do not feel guilty as much as I feel a deep sense of loss and disconnectedness—like I've missed out on something. My family doesn't respect me because of my reputation or position but simply because they love me. I shed my roles as pastor and board member in exchange for the role of husband and dad.

Over the last week I've engaged in wonderful conversations with excellent and hospitable people, and I have eaten some fine meals, ranging from pork roast to pizza, from lobster to lasagna. But tonight I'm eating with my family at home where we will talk and laugh, perhaps even weep and disagree. But I know that even if the main dish turns out to be baked broccoli, it will be a wonderful meal.

—Steve McKinley

REFLECTION

Where will I eat dinner tonight?

PRAYER

When I sit down to dinner tonight, Lord, may the plates be filled with love.

"What time will you be home for dinner?"

—My spouse

FAMILY

Ordering Priorities

You husbands must love your wives. . . . And now a word to you fathers. Don't make your children angry by the way you treat them.

EPHESIANS 5:25; 6:4

THE home is the toughest environment of all for leaders. Why is it the ones we love most are the ones we are most impatient with? My wife has often said to me, "I wish you were as patient with your children as you are with your constituents." She's right. She reminds me that I'm accountable to God and to my family, and I'm grateful for that.

I think the greatest problem is our allocation of time, whether or not we let our professions exclude time with our families. If our lives are going to be given only to our professions, then better we had remained as Paul said, unencumbered by marriage and family. But if we do decide to marry and have a family, I am thoroughly convinced one has to set priorities as follows:

First, God. The Bible teaches us to love the Lord with all our strength, mind, and heart. Our second priority is our families because they are the gift of God to us; they are the joint effort of God's creating authority working through us. Our third priority is our professions, and if we put our jobs anyplace higher than third place, we have our priorities askew.

I've tried to communicate to my family that no matter how busy I am, I am always accessible to them. We need to communicate that verbally but also by our actions.

—Mark Hatfield

REFLECTION

What does my allocation of time say about my priorities?

PRAYER

Lord Jesus, help me to take my family as seriously as you take the family of God.

"By profession I am a soldier and take pride in that fact. But I am prouder—infinitely prouder—to be a father."

—Douglas MacArthur, American five-star general, World War II

LEADERSHIP

A Heart for Others

*He is the one who gave these gifts
to the church: the apostles, the
prophets, the evangelists, and the
pastors and teachers. Their
responsibility is to equip God's
people to do his work and build
up the church, the body of Christ,
until we come to such unity in our
faith and knowledge of God's Son
that we will be mature and full
grown in the Lord, measuring up
to the full stature of Christ.*

EPHESIANS 4:11-13

EVERYWHERE I've served I've prayed for God to send me leaders to build his church. For fourteen years, at least once every month or so I'd meet someone who was visiting Skyline Church (my former pastorate) for the first time. We'd introduce ourselves. Then God would speak to me and say, *John, there's one.* That was the most humbling thing in life because I didn't do one thing to bring that person in.

After I resigned, I was with about seventy-five church leaders one night for a farewell dinner. I got up and said, "All my life I've prayed for leaders. Let me tell how God answered those prayers with you."

Then I went around the room, telling each one about the time we met, when God revealed, "There's one." By the time I was done, we were all bawling.

Someone said, "How could you remember meeting everyone in a church this size?"

I replied, "I don't remember meeting every person. I remember meeting *you* because you were one of those people I prayed God would lead into my life."

—John Maxwell

67

REFLECTION

Who are the leaders God has led into my life? How am I supposed to nurture them?

PRAYER

Lord, give me eyes to see all the gifts you bring into my life, including the gift of men and women whom you've called me to develop as leaders.

"One of the marks of true greatness is the ability to develop greatness in others."

—J. C. Macaulay (1889–1977),
writer and theologian

LEADERSHIP

What Do Leaders Do?

When they had assembled at Mizpah, they drew water and poured it out before the Lord. On that day they fasted and there they confessed, "We have sinned against the Lord." And Samuel was leader of Israel at Mizpah.

1 SAMUEL 7:6, NIV

THERE is nothing worse than learning how to play the game only to find that once you know how, someone has changed the rules. That is exactly what happened to Curtis. After ten years in leadership he was now the moderator of the church board. He knew that the role of boards was changing. Instead of keeping pastors in check, board members were to be the pastor's cheerleaders and protectors. Curtis knew he understood the change; however, he was not sure the rest of the board did. How would he lead his peers to change the way they had previously related to pastoral leadership?

In the only chapter describing Samuel's leadership (1 Sam. 7), Curtis found answers to his questions. First Samuel 7:6 says that Samuel was Israel's leader that day. The text reveals that being "leader" was more role than position.

First, Samuel both served and confronted his people. For twenty years Israel had been living in apostasy, and Samuel challenged their unfaithfulness.

Samuel also understood that it was the people's job to fight and it was his responsibility to pray. When Israel won the battle against the Philistines, Samuel erected a monument celebrating God's victory. Leaders are constantly looking for people who get it right and serve God well. Upon finding such people, leaders tell their stories as monuments to God's workings.

Finally, Samuel kept at it year after year.

So did Curtis. The board changed, but not overnight. It took time, patience, courage, and wisdom. Curtis learned to lead his board—confronting, praying, celebrating, and persevering—that is, by learning to do what leaders do.

—Paul Borden

71

REFLECTION

Which of these elements of Samuel's leadership—confronting, praying, celebrating, and persevering—do I need to grow in most?

PRAYER

God, show me areas in which I need to grow and develop in order to be an effective leader. And grant me a teachable heart.

"Leaders are ordinary people with extraordinary determination."

—Anonymous

⌐ LOVE FOR THE OUTCAST

....

Inconvenient Opportunity

A Jewish man was traveling on a
trip from Jerusalem to Jericho,
and he was attacked by bandits.
They stripped him of his clothes
and money, beat him up, and left
him half dead beside the road. . . .
Then a despised Samaritan came
along, and when he saw the man,
he felt deep pity.

LUKE 10:30-33

I WAS on a plane from Chicago to Milwaukee. I had asked for a seat with an empty seat beside it because I had a writing assignment and I needed to spread out my Bible and notes. So on this small plane I ended up being the only person with an empty seat next to her.

I got out my Bible, and just as we were about to take off, into the plane came a huge man, six feet four or six feet five—very masculine. But he was dressed like a woman—miniskirt and stockings, high-heeled white shoes and purse, and a wig. As this cross-dresser came down the aisle, I realized, *The only open seat is next to me. He's going to be sitting next to me all during this flight.* And I suddenly wanted to put my Bible away.

I'm amazed I had these reactions. Prejudices I didn't know I had came out. I said to the Lord, *I don't really care about him. I really don't care if he goes to heaven or hell. And that's the truth.* Here I was writing and preaching about these things, and suddenly here was a real-life human being, and I didn't care a bit about him.

I repented and said, *I'm sorry, Lord. Forgive me, and give me your heart for this man. You died for him.* I didn't lead him to Christ, but I didn't put my Bible away either. I smiled at him and changed my attitude. I began to ask myself, *What has happened in his life to bring him to this point?* And at the end of the journey, I had a compassion for him that I didn't have at the beginning.

—Jill Briscoe

REFLECTION

Who in my life might be like the man on the plane—and what does God want me to do for this person?

PRAYER

Lord of mercy, Lord of compassion, make me like you.

"Let my heart be broken by the things that break the heart of God."

—Bob Pierce, founder of World Vision

76

20

MARRIAGE

Were the Puritans Really Puritanical?

Let your wife be a fountain of blessing for you. Rejoice in the wife of your youth. She is a loving doe, a graceful deer. Let her breasts satisfy you always. May you always be captivated by her love.

PROVERBS 5:18-19

I CHUCKLE when people lambaste the Puritans for supposedly being sexually inhibited. The so-called puritanical attitude toward sex was actually quite progressive, overturning the more repressive notions that had dominated the church for at least a thousand years. One church leader, Ambrose, argued that "married people ought to blush at the state in which they are living." The church fathers Origen and Chrysostom believed that Adam and Eve could not have had sexual relations before the Fall. Therefore, if sin had not entered the world, the human race would reproduce itself by some means other than through intercourse. Eventually the church prohibited married couples from having sex on about half the days of the year. Some leaders recommended abstinence on five days out of seven every week.

But the Puritans changed all this. When they taught from the Bible on marriage, they affirmed the goodness of marital sex. In fact, scholar Leland Ryken has documented a case in which a New England congregation excommunicated a husband who shirked his sexual responsibilities to his wife. Frustrated by her husband's refusal to engage in sexual intimacy with her, she complained to her pastor and then to her church family.

Proverbs 5:18-19 endorses a robust sex life for

married couples. The sage captures the exquisite grace of a woman by comparing her to a doe. Then, in words that may cause a blush or two, he prays that the wife's breasts may satisfy her husband and that he may be captivated by her love. The word *captivated* in this case actually means "intoxicated" in the original—so this is the one passage where Scripture condones intoxication!

Sexual intimacy is a wonderful gift that God gives to husbands and wives, and the only thing that takes priority over it is intimacy with God himself. According to 1 Corinthians 7:5, spouses should not "deprive each other of sexual relations. The only exception to this rule would be the agreement of both husband and wife to refrain from sexual intimacy for a limited time, so they can give themselves more completely to prayer." As this verse suggests, couples have the privilege and responsibility of giving one another the gift of themselves in sexual intimacy.

—Steve Mathewson

REFLECTION

What can I do to enrich the sexual relationship I have with my spouse?

PRAYER

God, thank you for giving me _____ to be my spouse. May our marriage always be a means of honoring and glorifying you, and may we grow in grace with each other.

"Most Christian couples have never been taught what the Bible actually says about sex, nor, from the medical standpoint, how to fully enjoy what God has designed for man and wife."

—Ed Wheat, physician and author

21

MENTORING

The Greatest Investment

*You have heard me teach many
things that have been confirmed
by many reliable witnesses. Teach
these great truths to trustworthy
people who are able to pass them
on to others.*
2 TIMOTHY 2:2

O KAY, kid, let's see what you've got." Richard seized my black cardboard portfolio and tossed it onto the paint-splattered table. He shot a dubious glance toward me, then opened the portfolio and began to leaf through pages from my freshman figure-drawing course. Except for an occasional grunt, Richard didn't utter a word.

It was my first college internship as an art major. I believed Richard was skeptical of the whole endeavor, but because of his friendship with my dad, he had agreed to take me on. For the month of January I'd be living in a room off the garage behind his house in Los Angeles and driving with him to the studio, where I'd spend twelve hours a day priming canvases for his paintings and helping him create large cast-paper pieces. I respected his art and wanted him to see potential in me. I seriously hoped I would not embarrass myself.

The papers sighed as Richard closed the portfolio. I reddened when he turned and walked away without a word. Crossing the studio, he pulled a large brown-paper package off a shelf and came back, letting the heavy, flat package drop to the table with a crack.

"Kid, if you can draw like that, you have to

start using better paper. There's nothing better than this—rag paper from France, two dollars a sheet. From now on you'll use this." Then he returned to the collage he was composing. By the end of the month-long internship, he would end up investing in me much more than expensive rag paper—also the resources of his time, friendship, reputation, and insight.

In the union of divine purpose and human frailty, God shapes us into the likeness of his Son. He uses people to stretch us, to encourage us, and to lend accountability. A friend older in the faith can see possibilities in us where we see only ineffectual lines on a sheet of paper. Progress in the Christian life comes when we risk relationships with fellow believers who help us bring the picture into fuller dimension.

The apostle Paul knew that. The New Testament letters to Timothy reflect the elder-brotherly concern Paul felt for his young friend. He invested in Timothy, just as he knew Timothy would in turn do for others. The risk was worth it for Paul. It's worth it for us to seek mentors and to be mentors.

—Randal C. Working

REFLECTION

Who mentors me? What, if anything, makes me
hesitate to risk mentoring another?

PRAYER

Dear God, you have made yourself more real to
me through the investment of others in my life.
Provide people who will shape me more into your
likeness, and lead me to others for whom I can
make a difference.

*"We must discipline ourselves to be available—physi-
cally and emotionally—to one another. . . . [Most]
relationships feel like intrusions or interruptions instead
of being enjoyed as gifts or, even more, being celebrated as one of life's highest purposes."*

—Douglas Rumford, author

84

MENTORING

Helping Hands along the Way

*He is the one who gave these gifts
to the church: the apostles, the
prophets, the evangelists, and the
pastors and teachers. Their
responsibility is to equip God's
people to do his work and build
up the church, the body of Christ,
until we come to such unity in our
faith and knowledge of God's Son
that we will be mature and full
grown in the Lord, measuring up
to the full stature of Christ.*

EPHESIANS 4:11-13

I USED to think leadership was about being the person out in front, about being the one with all the answers. I was so wrong. As I reflect on how I grew from the woman in the pew to a leader in ministry, I realize how blessed I was to have so many patient, loving, tenacious people assist me on that journey. All were different, and yet each left thumbprints on my identity as a leader.

A man named Charles equipped me by asking the right questions. Often the questions were, What do you need from me? How can I support you? But his style of drawing out my leadership gift came in the form of questions and challenges. If I came seeking advice about a concern, he would say, "Sue, see this as your ministry challenge. How are you going to handle it? Have you taken time to pray about it?" Charles brought out the learner in me.

Bill taught me how to rely on my faith. With every new challenge I faced personally or professionally, Bill taught me about the challenges of Jesus and Paul. In times of fear and darkness he reminded me that I was not alone and helped me claim the Word as my single greatest survival skill. Bill taught me about the power of reflection and,

by his supportive teaching style, helped me see
that Christ is in each and every one of us.

Nancy helped me to grow through her
encouragement. She supported my dreams with
prayers, ideas, and actions. Nancy taught me
about advocacy, that leaders need to speak the
truth in love, to never remain silent and allow
injustice. Nancy supported me by challenging me
to be a good steward of my health, both spiritual
and physical, and my boundaries, both personal
and professional. She equipped me with her love
and her wisdom, but most of all by her character
and by what she modeled.

Brad taught me about integrity, truth, and
grace. His humility reminded me of Jesus' teaching that as leaders we are first of all servants. And
his humor affirmed again and again that ministry
is really fun.

None of my mentors told me what to do or
how to do it. Yet they each supported my growth
in very different ways. I have learned many things
on my journey, mostly through my mistakes. But
my greatest lesson is that God continues to use the
seemingly unqualified to do the unimaginable.

—Sue Mallory

REFLECTION

Who has been the greatest influence in my life and why? What kind of equipper am I—"power over" or "support under"?

PRAYER

Gracious and loving God, I give you thanks for continuing to bless my life with teachers, equippers, and mentors who lead from a support position and allow me to risk, to fail, and to grow in the challenges. Father, as I seek to help others to grow, help me to remember not to tell but to ask and listen so that they may discover and grow in their own very special gifts.

"An authentic leader acts in ways which serve to elevate those around him."

—Sean M. Georges

23

OBEDIENCE

Teresa's Dream

*[Jesus'] mother told the servants,
"Do whatever he tells you."*

TERESA was a single mom with a dream. All her life people had told her that she was an entrepreneur. As a little girl she played store, ran the lemonade stand on the block, and organized the other children to play her games. Her dream was to start a business that would fulfill her gifting, help her support her children, and touch the lives of people in both redemptive and creative ways.

Teresa faced numerous obstacles. She was committed to the spiritual, moral, and intellectual development of her children. She felt she needed to be fiscally responsible with her funds. And single moms with two children often find it difficult to get the financing they need to start a new business. She was convinced her plan was from God, and yet to implement it in obedience to him would not be easy.

Teresa faced the same tension David encountered in 2 Samuel 8. He had become king of a conquered nation, and therefore, he fought battle after battle to achieve independence for Israel. As he gained each victory, he did two things. First, he hamstrung the horses. This made them incapable of pulling all the chariots being collected in victory. Second, he took much of the gold and silver he recovered in victory and put it into an irrevocable trust dedicated to Jehovah. This made it impossible to use this resource to finance more battles. David did these two things in obedience to God, who said that kings were not to collect horses and wealth, in order that their trust might be in him (Deut. 17).

Such obedience put David at great risk—so much so that when he fought both the Arameans and Edomites, he thought he would lose this two-front war (Ps. 60). Instead, God came to his aid in the Valley of Salt, and David became king of a conquering, not a conquered, nation. God was honored when David obeyed to the point of risk.

Teresa chose to follow the pattern of David. She risked everything, including her house, to start the business. The first year was so difficult that she lost her home. But then the business took off. It not only enabled her to touch many people, but the whole experience became an opportunity for her children to grow and develop.

Certainly we are called to be prudent stewards of what God has given us, and such bold risk taking isn't for everyone. But we are also called to do whatever Jesus tells us—even when the outcome is uncertain.

—Paul Borden

91

REFLECTION

Has God given me a dream that is requiring some risk from me?

PRAYER

Lord, help me to discern between foolish risk and obedience that does not count the cost.

"The eagle that soars in the upper air does not worry itself how it is to cross rivers."

—Gladys Aylward (1902–1970),
English missionary to China

24

OPPORTUNITY

No Empty Time

*We live our lives beneath your
wrath. We end our lives with a
groan.*

*Seventy years are given to us!
Some may even reach eighty. But
even the best of these years are
filled with pain and trouble; soon
they disappear, and we are
gone. . . . Teach us to make the
most of our time, so that we may
grow in wisdom.*

PSALM 90:9-10, 12

A PORTION of Scripture that guides me constantly is 2 Peter 3:8, where Peter says, "A day is like a thousand years to the Lord, and a thousand years is like a day."

I believe that every moment is an opportunity to be seized. Each day is as a thousand years; our twenty-four-hour slice of time is a sunrise-to-sunset opportunity for us to do something, by the grace of God, that counts for eternity. Everything we do here has a direct bearing on what's going to happen there. When I think about it, it makes me not want to waste my moments but to redeem the time, to seize the opportunity.

A French mystic of the seventeenth century said that God does not give us time in which to do nothing. There is no such thing as empty time. Now, certainly there must be times of rest and respite in which you go before the Lord in solitude. But even our meditation has a beautiful purpose, a sweet repose in which those moments of rest benefit the soul and end up glorifying God. This perspective makes even our suffering purposeful.

It doesn't mean we're any less busy—it may mean we're more busy. But the load is lightened knowing that this translates out to eternity—in our life, in another's life, and for the glory of God.

—Joni Eareckson Tada

REFLECTION

Do I have the right kind of busyness in my life?

PRAYER

Lord, help me to employ my time for you, not in frantic busyness, as if I had something to prove to you, but in calm thankfulness for all you've given me, including the gift of time.

"I have this minute in my control. It is all I really do have to work with. It is as magnificent or drab or vile as the thoughts which fill it. I fear our most common sin is empty minutes."

—Frank Laubach, late missionary and author

25

OUTREACH

Go Sow Those Oats

*Some seeds fell on fertile soil and
produced a crop that was thirty,
sixty, and even a hundred times as
much as had been planted.*

MATTHEW 13:8

WHEN I was nine, the most adventurous place I knew was my grandparents' cow barn. My cousins and I played hide-and-seek in the haymow, carefully avoiding the terrifying trapdoors. We caught mice in the silo; the one who caught the most would win. Or we would force the kittens into doll clothes and make them play house with us. In the end, their mewling impelled us to free them of their straitjackets.

One day we found a room we'd never seen before. There was a ladder nailed to a sturdy wall. We ventured up and looked over the edge. Oats! I remember the smell of them, the fuzziness their dust gave in the sunbeams from the loft window. We climbed into them, invading the loft with our laughter and rustling. We created new games there, hiding a softball in the oat mountain to see if someone could find it. As I lay very still, my cousins covered all but my face. The oats swaddled me in a prenatal warmth and coziness.

When we heard the dinner bell, we ran to the sunporch, yanked off our shoes, shook the oats out of them, and slapped away the chaff. Grandpa had seen us coming up the sidewalk and had figured where we had been. "Kids," he said, with warning in his voice, "the oats you found are my seed oats. They are not for playing! They are for planting!" He was a man who rarely got angry—I still remember his face.

"A sower went out to sow." Some of us would rather stay in the coziness of the seed barn than go out into the field. There is no risk that our seed will be eaten by birds, scorched by hot wind, or strangled by thistles. But the seeds of the kingdom of heaven, the gospel of our Lord, the gifts of grace gathered inside the walls of the church are not meant to stay inside those walls. They are meant for planting.

Our geographic locations, relationships, job opportunities, prayer lives, and leadership roles are all means of readying the soil for planting. Yes, we will encounter hard ground and harder hearts, dry ground and drier spirits, tenacious weeds and rapacious birds. But sowers go out to sow. Planting with best efforts, freely, fully, investing the precious seed for future growth, is where the gospel adventure starts.

—Mary C. Miller

REFLECTION

Where have I sown even a tiny seed of the gospel today?

PRAYER

Jesus, forgive me for hoarding such a treasure, and help me to go out and sow joyfully and energetically, trusting that your Spirit will do the rest.

"There is a subtle false teaching that says we can be evangelical without being evangelistic. It has us believe we 'go' to church rather than we 'are' the church."

—Chris A. Lyons, pastor

100

26

⌒ OUTREACH

Keep It Personal

*Jesus now called the Twelve and
gave them authority and power to
deal with all the demons and cure
diseases. He commissioned them to
preach the news of God's kingdom
and heal the sick. He said,
"Don't load yourselves up with
equipment. Keep it simple; you
are the equipment."*

LUKE 9:1-3, *The Message*

VIRTUALLY every business claims, "Our people are our most important asset." In many cases that statement has little to do with reality. Scott Adams has tapped into our national frustration with work with his syndicated cartoon strip, *Dilbert.* Inept management, confusing mission statements, misfit coworkers, and insufficient resources to do the job define the workplace in Dilbert's world, and apparently, two hundred million readers worldwide find that it defines theirs as well.

In one cartoon Dilbert explains to his friend Wally that empowerment is a secret buzzword management uses to mean "designating someone to blame." That kind of cynicism may be warranted in some places of work, but not in Christ's kingdom.

In today's passage Jesus empowered his disciples, making it clear that they were his only means of carrying out his God-given mission. Is that still true in the technological age?

Today we have the potential to touch billions of lives through satellites and Web sites. But technology is merely the conduit by which Christ followers share how he has changed their lives. There is no more powerful message, no more powerful tool than a transformed life that is diligently pursuing the agenda and priorities of God's kingdom.

Sharing our faith with others becomes a daunting task when we turn it into a sales presentation. If we believe we must memorize dozens of verses of Scripture and (three, four, or is it five?) spiritual laws while simultaneously being prepared to counter every intellectual argument, most of us will never be a part of seeing someone come to faith.

But anyone can work to right wrongs. Anyone can serve the needy. And anyone can tell the simple story of how God in Christ changed his heart. When we do these things, we find ourselves doing evangelism the way Jesus did evangelism.

Jesus did not give this empowerment just to the professional clergy with seminary degrees. He did not give it just to the extroverted or those who think well on their feet. He gave it to all Christ followers. We have a clear sense of our responsibility. We have been given both authority and power to share Christ's message. But we have also been filled by the Holy Spirit and given spiritual gifts so that together we can move toward the accomplishment of our mission.

Let's keep the mission simple. Let's keep the mission central. Let's keep the mission personal.

—Ed Rowell

REFLECTION

Am I clear about my specific role in my organization's mission? Am I lacking in the area of "how-to" or in the area of "want-to"?

PRAYER

Lord, how can I become better equipped or motivated so that I may serve you with greater effectiveness?

"Preach the gospel at all times. If necessary, use words."

—St. Francis of Assisi

OUTREACH

Overcoming the Outreach Hurdles

*Though I am free and belong to
no man, I make myself a slave to
everyone, to win as many as
possible. . . . I have become all
things to all men so that by all
possible means I might save some.*
1 CORINTHIANS 9:19, 22, NIV

THREE months ago I attended a meeting of ten people who meet twice a week for lunch. My sole purpose for going was outreach, and I went with the goal of joining these people at least once a month.

For me that gathering had a host of negatives. My commute lasted an hour and a half each way. I sat next to someone who smoked throughout the meal. The lowest priced sandwich on the menu was eight dollars. Much of the table conversation did not interest me.

Two weeks later I rejoined this group for lunch, but to my regret I haven't been there since.

I don't know anyone who would say outreach is easy. Exhilarating, yes; easy, no. Reaching out is difficult for many reasons, but in 1 Corinthians 9 Paul identifies one of the most fundamental: To reach out to others requires sacrifice. We must be unselfish if we are to risk rejection or give up our time and money on an unsure result. The hurdle keeping me from the luncheon has been an unwillingness to sacrifice.

What can motivate us to go against our self-interest to reach those outside the church? According to 1 Corinthians 9, two things:

The first, obviously, is the passionate desire to "save some." While this is obvious, it is not something I gladly keep in mind. Because the thought of anyone's going to hell is so terrible, I can easily avoid the thought and ignore what is at stake for people without Christ. If I am willing to sacrifice my mental comfort, though, the destiny of people without Christ will help me pay a high price for their sakes.

The second thing that helps us overcome self-interest is spiritual self-interest. Paul, on the heels of his unselfish words about being a slave to all, says, "I do all this for the sake of the gospel, *that I may share in its blessings*" (1 Cor. 9:23, NIV, italics added).

Paul says he receives a huge personal gain from all his sacrifice. The message of Christ overflows with spiritual riches for all who become its servants. Serving the gospel is like serving a customer who is an extraordinarily lavish tipper. In the end, you receive far more than you give.

—Craig Brian Larson

REFLECTION

What is the biggest hurdle of self-interest I must overcome to increase my outreach?

PRAYER

Lord, help me to sacrifice my own comfort and convenience for the sake of those who need to know you.

"If you live by the same values and priorities Jesus had, you will find evangelism happening naturally. It becomes a lifestyle and not a project."

—Rebecca Manley Pippert, author

PERSEVERANCE

The First Abolitionist

*I am counting on the Lord; yes, I
am counting on him. I have put
my hope in his word. I long for
the Lord more than sentries long
for the dawn, yes, more than
sentries long for the dawn.*

*O Israel, hope in the Lord; for
with the Lord there is unfailing
love and an overflowing supply
of salvation.*

PSALM 130:5-7

THE slave trade in the late 1700s involved thousands of Africans, hundreds of ships, and millions of British pounds; upon it depended the economies of Britain and much of Europe. Yet few were aware of the horrors of the so-called Middle Passage across the Atlantic, where an estimated one out of four Africans died. And those who were aware didn't think it possible to do anything about a system so entrenched in the culture and economy.

The exception was a small band of activists, mostly Christian, that included William Wilberforce, a member of Parliament with a gentle grin and a small, twisted body.

Upon his conversion in 1786, Wilberforce had written in his journal, "My walk is a public one. My business is in the world, and I must mix in the assemblies of men." Not long after that Wilberforce became increasingly disturbed about the slave trade and determined that its abolition was one of his life's great purposes. Later he reflected, "So enormous, so dreadful, so irremediable did the trade's wickedness appear that my own mind was completely made up for abolition. Let the consequences be what they would."

In May 1788 Wilberforce, with the help of researcher Thomas Clarkson, introduced a twelve-point motion to Parliament indicting the slave trade. The motion was defeated, but Wilberforce was not. His campaign intensified, and so did the opposition. Planters, businessmen, ship owners, traditionalists, and even the Crown stood against him and viewed abolitionists like him as dangerous radicals. But even they couldn't deny his perseverance: As one Jamaican agent wrote, "It is necessary to watch him, as he is blessed with a very sufficient quantity of that enthusiastic spirit, which is so far from yielding that it grows more vigorous from blows." He was right. In 1791 Wilberforce introduced another anti-slave-trade bill, which was also defeated. Defeats of further motions followed in 1792, 1793, 1797, 1798, 1799, 1804, and 1805.

But slowly abolitionist efforts turned the tide of public opinion, and in 1806 Parliament relented and abolished the slave trade throughout the British Empire. Wilberforce wept with joy.

Not willing to rest on his laurels, he next sought the abolition of slavery itself. Though age and illness forced his retirement from that battle, he did see a victory twenty-six years later: Parliament abolished slavery throughout the British Empire.

—Mark Galli

REFLECTION

In what areas am I now tempted to give up? In which of these am I called to persevere?

PRAYER

Lord, help me to discern those obstacles that indicate I should abandon the project, as well as those that are calling me to exercise more faith and perseverance.

"Every noble work is at first impossible."

—Thomas Carlyle (1795–1881),
Scottish historian and essayist

29

PLANNING

No Good Substitute

Commit your work to the Lord,
and then your plans will succeed.
PROVERBS 16:3

I HAVE always been impressed with how people in the Bible planned strategically as they sought to carry out the mission of God:

- Moses appointed officials over the people of Israel and had them serve as judges.
- David planned and provided for the building of the temple and left everything needed for Solomon to complete the task.
- Nehemiah made careful preparation and plans for the rebuilding of the walls of Jerusalem in order to restore security and self-esteem to the people of Israel after the Babylonian captivity.
- As the time approached for Jesus to complete his mission, he set his face like a flint toward Jerusalem. It was as if Christ had orchestrated the events of his final days on earth in order to accomplish God's divine plan.
- The apostle Paul developed a missionary strategy of proclaiming the gospel and establishing churches in centers of commerce from which believers could take the gospel to outlying villages.

Throughout biblical history godly people have

been strategic planners. Prayerful and thoughtful analysis and preparation are the keys in designing for success in the work of God. The five phases of effective planning include: (1) analysis, which asks, "Where are we?" (2) vision, which asks, "Where are we going?" (3) planning, which asks, "How are we going to get there?" (4) funding, which asks, "How are we going to pay for it?" and (5) implementation, which asks, "How are we doing?"

The purpose of strategic planning is to create a set of priorities that enable us to act courageously and responsibly today to advance toward the future with a greater expression of God's work in the world. It is an intentional effort to seek the inspiration and guidance of the Holy Spirit in order to discern the will of God as we move into the future.

My experience as a preacher is that the Holy Spirit often moves just as well in the quiet of my study as he does in the pulpit; there is no substitute for good planning and preparation. As Solomon once wrote, "Where there is no revelation, the people cast off restraint" (Prov. 29:18, NIV).

—Peter Barnes

115

REFLECTION

What area of my life or ministry do I need to be more strategic about?

PRAYER

Lord, help me not only to know what I'm to do, but give me the energy and will to do it strategically, faithfully, and persistently.

"Four steps to achievement: Plan purposefully, prepare prayerfully, proceed positively, pursue persistently."

—William Arthur Ward, inspirational writer

116

30

POWER

Power Watch

Who else among the gods is like you, O Lord? Who is . . . like you—so awesome in splendor, performing such wonders?

EXODUS 15:11

MOST of us have been in the presence of the powerful at one time or another. Whether the power is that of wealth or spiritual influence or political will, we know it when we see it.

When I was eleven years old, I went with a Salvation Army officer to a luncheon with Billy Graham. I have a press photo of me, a nerdy kid with glasses, shaking hands with the man who has preached the gospel to more people than anyone else in history.

When I was thirteen, I attended the church where then-governor Ronald Reagan occasionally worshiped. You could tell the Sundays he was there: A cadre of bodyguards spaced themselves throughout the sanctuary. In their black suits and earphones they stood out from the casually dressed California worshipers like crows in a flock of seagulls.

When I was twenty-one and a student in Paris, my brother and I went to the Champs-Elysées one bright June day to watch Pope John Paul II pass by. Newspapers reported that a million people lined the boulevard to catch a glimpse of the pope as he waved to the people.

Persons of great power might seem like abstractions. Their influence is far beyond what most of us can imagine. And what of those who abuse power? The litany of their names is imprinted upon our minds, from crooked politicians to self-serving stars to the tyrants of history.

The Bible has much to say about the mighty and the influential, about those who exercise authority or dominion. The bottom line: They are accountable to God.

God, who alone is omnipotent, gives those of vast influence their power as a trust from him. The defining experience of Israel was the exodus from Egypt, a great expression of God's power in the face of abusive human power. Since Pharaoh did not use his power to protect the people in his care, he came face-to-face with God's judgment. The manifestation of God's power contrasts starkly with the power hungry and the ambitious. God uses his strength not to oppress but to liberate, not to abuse but to save.

That's a lesson for us ordinary people as well. In contrast to seeking our own acclaim or privilege, God invites us to use any influence we have, whether impressive or not, to serve others in the name of the One who holds all power and authority.

—Randal C. Working

119

REFLECTION

How do I covet power, and how can I use whatever power I have to serve others for Jesus' sake?

PRAYER

Father, thank you that your same power that created the universe expressed itself in self-giving love on the cross.

"The only cure for the love of power is the power of love."

—Sherri McAdam

120

31

RESPONSIBILITY

Men Not Working

If you just listen and don't obey, it is like looking at your face in a mirror but doing nothing to improve your appearance. You see yourself, walk away, and forget what you look like.

JAMES 1:23-24

ONE day as I was driving to work, I noticed two city trucks filled with road tar near an intersection notorious for potholes. Since I had managed to hit at least one pothole a day for the last several weeks, I was delighted to see the city finally addressing this problem. The traffic light was red, so I had a couple of minutes to observe the city crew who presumably had been sent out for the job. What I noticed was that during the entire cycle of the light, none of the five workmen moved. Three of them were leaning on their shovels.

Out of curiosity I decided to drive around the block again to see if they were going to get to work. Several minutes and two red lights later, the crew still hadn't started the job. They hadn't even moved! This was confirming all my suspicions regarding government employees. So I went around the block yet again to see how long the five could keep from working . . . and returned to the same picture.

Irritated, I wanted to get out of the car and confront those irresponsible workers or at least call city hall and complain about my high taxes' paying for their potholed streets. But I checked my watch and realized I needed to be at work for an early morning appointment. I arrived at the office ten minutes late and apologized to the man who had been impatiently waiting for me, explaining the reason for my delay. In becoming consumed by someone else's irresponsibility, I became irresponsible.

We each have a personal mission in life, but often we do not fulfill that mission because we are worrying about others who aren't fulfilling theirs. When we turn our attention away from what God has called us to do in order to fixate on the flaws of others, we are not only being irresponsible; we are turning away from God. May our testimony be that of the psalmist: "For I have kept the ways of the Lord; I have not done evil by turning from my God" (Ps. 18:21, NIV).

—Gary Fenton

123

REFLECTION

Do I worry too much about what others leave undone and not enough about my own short-comings?

PRAYER

God, keep my eyes on the path you have planned for me today instead of on the pathways of others.

"While no man has succeeded . . . without some spark of divine fire, many have succeeded better by taking precious good care of a precious small spark than others, who have been careless with a generous flame."

—Henry Holt

124

⤳ REST

···

Go Get Some Sleep!

*Jesus said, "Let's get away from
the crowds for a while and rest."
There were so many people
coming and going that Jesus and
his apostles didn't even have time
to eat.*

MARK 6:31

A RECENT Internet pass-around had the heading "Signs you've had too much of the '90s." Several of these "signs" give evidence that we tend to ignore Jesus' words regarding rest:

- You have a "to-do list" that includes entries for lunch and bathroom breaks, and they are usually the ones that never get crossed off.
- You get all excited when it's Saturday and you can wear sweats to work.
- You think working a "half-day" means leaving at five o'clock.

Working long hours and not getting enough sleep are so common that we no longer consider them liabilities. We brag about them to one another. We never stop to consider the spiritual impact of contemporary work and leisure habits.

Scientists tell us that before the invention of electric lights, most people slept an average of ten hours per night. Today, we average less than seven-and-a-half hours. Many of the health problems that we face today are directly related to a lack of sleep, yet we doggedly attempt to squeeze a little more out of each day. What we discover is that in our quest to do more and be more, we often create such a high degree of stress that we cannot sleep when we get the chance!

In the passage above, Jesus had just learned that his cousin, John the Baptist, had been killed. Even the Son of God experienced the limitations of the human body when faced with grief, hunger, and too many demands. By his example he taught the disciples to minister effectively over the long haul by taking care of their physical needs.

Somehow, we must come to believe the words of Jesus and learn to create time and space for rest and quiet. Just as stress and fatigue put a damper on marital intimacy, they create a real barrier to our spiritual intimacy as well.

127

Time-management experts often recommend keeping a time log in order to identify wasted time. Their goal is to redeem that time for productive work. But the same exercise could also be used to redeem time for rest and recreation. Instead of giving in to the cultural expectations to do more, we can focus on those spiritual disciplines that lead us to *be* more.

—Ed Rowell

REFLECTION

What if I adjusted my bedtime backwards by fifteen minutes this week—and then by another fifteen minutes next week? What would I lose? What would I gain?

PRAYER

Lord, help me to remember that rest is necessary and productive, and a gift from you!

"Sometimes, the most spiritual thing we can do is take a nap."

—Richard Foster, writer

SERVANTHOOD

Our Money—or Our Lives?

[Jesus] sat down and called the twelve disciples over to him. Then he said, "Anyone who wants to be the first must take last place and be the servant of everyone else."

MARK 9:35

I T'S hard to glamorize the disciples of Jesus when you pay attention to the Scriptures. Today's passage is a response to their ongoing argument about who was the greatest among them. When Jesus asked them about it, they kept quiet out of embarrassment. His response offers the antidote for pride and ambition and a model for true leadership.

A few years ago, when Mother Teresa visited Phoenix, Arizona, to speak at the opening of a home for the destitute, KTAR, the largest radio station in town, interviewed her. During a commercial break the announcer asked Mother Teresa whether there was anything he could do for her. He expected her to request a donation or ask for media help to raise money for the new facility.

Instead, she looked him in the eye and said, "Yes, there is. Find someone nobody else loves and love them."

I've never heard the rest of the story. I don't know if the challenge of that diminutive nun from Calcutta caused that disc jockey to seek out someone to love unconditionally or not. But it is a challenge that's hard to ignore.

Giving a gift of money is never as costly as giving of our lives. The gift of money is immediate. But giving our lives is ongoing.

The gift of money represents that past portion of our lives that we have already invested in our work. The gift of service represents a desire to invest more of our future in that which has eternal significance. Once money leaves our hands, so often the memory of it leaves us as well. But when we give our hearts, the memories are with us forever.

While money is a necessary (and always appreciated!) ingredient for any kingdom endeavor, the most acute need is always for leaders and servants. Where are those who will invest themselves in the lives of others, nurturing, encouraging, and developing people into mature disciples? Most of us, if offered a choice between giving some extra money to our church or working in the church's preschool department, would dig deep into our pockets!

But it is precisely that sacrificial quality of service that makes it so valuable. Whether it is teaching children in Sunday school or being part of the work crew that puts a new roof on the crisis pregnancy center, serving is the key to keeping our priority and focus.

—Ed Rowell

131

REFLECTION

What are some of the unique experiences God has used to bring growth in my life? How can serving others redeem even difficult experiences?

PRAYER

God, please bring to mind people who would benefit from spending time with me. How could I offer them encouragement, hope, and opportunities to grow? Grant me the courage to contact them—*today.*

"The man who keeps busy helping the man below him won't have time to envy the man above him."

—Henrietta Mears, twentieth-century
Christian educator

SERVANTHOOD

Better Get Used to Being Used

I am among you as one who serves.
LUKE 22:27, NRSV

MARTIN Luther King Jr. did not want to go
to Memphis. The civil rights movement
was in trouble, splintering into feuding factions.
King was tired and overburdened. There were
many reasons not to go and support a floundering
garbage-workers' strike in Memphis.

But King went anyway. And his presence
infused new life into the strike.

"Each day strikers were giving up and going
back to work. We were discouraged. But when
Dr. King showed up, we knew that God was
with us and that we would win," said one of the
garbage workers.

The rest is history. King met his fate in a small
southern city, supporting a few hundred woefully
underpaid garbagemen.

In one sense it was a sad ending; in another
sense it was a fitting one. After all, King served
the crucified Messiah, who hung between two
thieves on a hill overlooking a garbage dump outside the big city.

Jesus reminds us that Christian service involves,
in the words of Henri Nouwen, "downward mobil-
ity." Our leadership is in our service.

At the Last Supper Jesus' disciples got into a
squabble over leadership. The people who had followed Jesus the most closely and heard all of his

teaching were still seeking preferential treatment, still lusting for places of honor at the banquet.

His response? "I am among you as one who serves," he told them.

Possibly the earliest designation for Christian leaders in the New Testament is *diakonos,* "deacon," which translated literally in English means "butler, waiter, servant." Never forget that whatever office we happen to hold in church, it is part of the diaconate. It is all part of servanthood, leadership by basin and towel.

The young seminarian was sliding chairs into place in the church fellowship hall. As my wife walked by, she heard the intern mutter aloud, "When will this church realize that I am a minister and not their congregational lackey? I went to seminary to move chairs?"

My wife commented in passing, "I think you already know the answer to your question. You are a minister; therefore, you are always somebody's lackey. We prefer to call it service or ministry, but you'll be moving chairs or setting tables or something like that to help somebody else's meeting with God. Better get used to being used."

The basin, the towel, the chairs, the garbage strike—that is servant leadership. That's how Christ would do it. —William Willimon

REFLECTION

What seemingly insignificant acts of service have I performed lately?

PRAYER

God, so many of the things I do in my work, in my family, and around church have little to do with status or education. Give me the grace to perform even the humblest task as unto you.

"A Christian who is ambitious to be a star disqualifies himself as a leader."

—David Watson

136

SERVANTHOOD

The Waitress Who Taught Me about "Deaconing"

They began to argue among themselves as to who would be the greatest in the coming Kingdom. Jesus told them, "In this world the kings and great men order their people around, and yet they are called 'friends of the people.' But among you, those who are the greatest should take the lowest rank, and the leader should be like a servant.

LUKE 22:24-26

I LEARNED about "deaconing" from my mother. She never held the office of deacon, but she showed me how it was done. When I was a child, every Friday and Saturday afternoon she waited tables at Pasquale's Italian Restaurant. She got home late, and usually the next morning I would discover a pizza in the refrigerator for Saturday morning breakfast. On Sunday morning she was up early to get us ready to go to Sunday school and worship together.

When I became a teenager, she got me a job as the dishwasher at Pasquale's. Soon I was promoted to busboy. I cleaned tables for all the servers, and I quickly learned that my mother was the best waitress in the place. She cared about the people at her tables—and they noticed. They tipped her accordingly, which mattered to me because servers shared their tips with busboys. If she had a good tipping night, so did I. And where did that hard-earned money she made on Friday and Saturday nights go? I'm guessing it helped her son go to college later on.

The Greek word for deaconing, the word used three times in Acts 6:1-6 where the order of deaconing is established, means "to serve or minister." Herodotus, a Greek historian who lived nearly five hundred years before Jesus, used it for "waiting on tables." It often referred to service commonly called "women's work." Jesus himself picked up this theme in Luke 22:24-27. There a dispute broke out among his closest followers about who was the greatest. Jesus said to them: "Who is greater, the one who is at the table or the one who serves? Is it not the one who is at the table? But I am among you as one who serves" (NIV)—which literally translates as "I am among you as a deacon."

Whether we're church professionals or lay leaders, up front or behind the scenes, we're all called to "deaconing"—to "waiting on tables" in Christ's name.

—Harry Heintz

REFLECTION

Whom might I serve in this way today?

PRAYER

Lord Christ, as the Redeemer of humanity, you bent to wash dirty feet. Give me a servant's heart, and help me to remember that I never stand taller than when I am stooping low to minister to another.

"If you are a Christian, then you are a minister. A non-ministering Christian is a contradiction in terms."

—Elton Trueblood (1900–1994), evangelical Quaker philosopher-theologian

SERVANTHOOD

How Low Can You Go?

Since I, the Lord and Teacher,
have washed your feet, you ought
to wash each other's feet.

JOHN 13:14

I REMEMBER a time when my father taught me something valuable about Christian leadership. Dad and I were padding through tall pines, our feet quiet on the carpet of brown pine needles. We had come to New Hampshire, just the two of us, something we had never done before. I knew then that I, a full eleven years old, was becoming a man.

We placed our net, tackle boxes, and rods in the canoe, then slipped it quietly into the Ossipee River. As Dad paddled from the back, I cast my trustworthy Mepps lure near the lily pads. Father, son, canoe, water, fish, pines—this was boyhood heaven. I desperately wanted to show Dad that I was worthy of the confidence he had placed in me by inviting me on this trip.

Two nights later I awoke painfully sick to my stomach. I feared I might throw up. I needed to get to the bathroom—now. But the cabin was cold and dark, and I would have to climb out of my warm top bunk. . . . Suddenly I threw up over the side.

My dad heard the awful splatter and came running in, clicked on the light, and surveyed the spreading mess. "Couldn't you have gotten to the bathroom?" he asked.

"I'm sorry," I said, knowing I deserved every

angry comment that would come. I had done something foolish, messy, embarrassing—and worst of all, childish.

But my dad didn't yell. He didn't call me names. He shook his head a little, then left and came back with a bucket of hot, sudsy water and a scrub brush. I watched amazed as he got down on hands and knees and began scrubbing each pine board clean again.

When Dad died suddenly eight years ago, he left me with that picture.

As Christian leaders we face many awful and embarrassing messes. Our people may often let us down. But Jesus has already shown us what we must do in those situations: "Since I, the Lord and Teacher, have washed your feet, you ought to wash each other's feet" (John 13:14).

—Kevin A. Miller

143

REFLECTION

Am I willing to bend down to "scrub the floor boards clean" when someone leaves me a disappointing mess?

PRAYER

Lord, as Jesus bent low to wash his disciples' feet, help me to serve those around me with grace and humility.

"If you wish to be a leader you will be frustrated, for very few people wish to be led. If you aim to be a servant, you will never be frustrated."

—Frank F. Warren

144

SIMPLICITY

Shedding the "Stuff"

Don't store up treasures here on earth, where they can be eaten by moths and get rusty, and where thieves break in and steal. Store your treasures in heaven, where they will never become moth-eaten or rusty and where they will be safe from thieves. Wherever your treasure is, there your heart and thoughts will also be.

MATTHEW 6:19-21

THE discipline of simplicity is not the most pleasant of spiritual disciplines, but it remains one of the most important. We so easily allow our lives to be defined by possessions, status, and all manner of social expectations. Being a disciple means shedding ourselves of anything that blurs our vision of Christ. No person better illustrates this than Francis of Assisi.

His father, Pietro, was a wealthy Italian cloth merchant, and he taught the adolescent Francis the family business. But when Francis entered his early twenties, he began to think his life was becoming too complicated, too concerned with status and wealth.

One day Francis impulsively took fine fabric from the family shop, rode to market, and sold it. Then he sold the family horse he'd been riding. And then—this is what infuriated Pietro—Francis gave away the proceeds to the poor! As if this weren't bad enough, a month later Pietro discovered Francis walking the streets of Assisi, begging for food and becoming a laughingstock. An enraged Pietro dragged Francis home, beat him, and locked him in a dark cellar, limiting him to bread and water until he came to his senses. When this punishment didn't work, he dragged Francis before the local bishop.

The bishop told Francis that it was not right to steal, even from one's family, or even if for the poor. He instructed Francis to return what he had taken. Francis looked shaken but said nothing. He simply stepped into an adjoining room while Pietro and the bishop waited.

Francis emerged a few minutes later, completely naked. Carrying his clothes in a neat pile, he walked up to Pietro and placed them at his feet. He then turned to those present and said, "Up to now, I have called Pietro di Bernardone father. Hereafter I shall not say, 'Father Pietro di Bernardone,' but 'Our Father Who Art in Heaven!'"

The bishop was so moved that he took off his cope and wrapped it around Francis, who just turned and walked out of the cathedral. It was a break with everything his father represented— comfort, wealth, status. Francis wanted nothing to stand in the way of his following Christ.

Few of us are called to make such radical breaks, but the larger point is still well taken. You don't have to be fabulously wealthy to see that material things can clutter the spiritual life and that periodically we must shed ourselves of some "stuff" so we can focus our lives on Christ again.

—Mark Galli

147

REFLECTION

How can I make my life less complicated, simpler, so that I have more time and energy to focus on things spiritual?

PRAYER

Lord, show me yourself afresh so that I can once again see and feel that you are more valuable than anything I can own or attain—so that I won't be so tempted to spend my energies accumulating things but rather living for you.

"The Christian discipline of simplicity is an inward reality that reflects an outward lifestyle. Both the inward and outward aspects of simplicity are essential."

—Richard Foster, author

148

SPIRITUAL GIFTS

Missing Genius

*Now there are different kinds of
spiritual gifts, but it is the same
Holy Spirit who is the source of
them all. There are different kinds
of service in the church, but it is
the same Lord we are serving.*

1 CORINTHIANS 12:4-5

THE computation of the sum total of IQs in Rockefeller Chapel was far beyond my mathematical abilities. This huge sanctuary was filled to overflowing with the educated elite that the world-class University of Chicago welcomes. Unamplified, a voice from the balcony behind us introduced the beautiful but extensive program, J. S. Bach's *The Passion according to Saint John.* Then he paused and added, "This evening, above all, is to give thanks to God for the indisputable genius of Johann Sebastian Bach and his gift to Christ's church."

It was a far cry from what the local city council recorded when Bach died. "Master Bach was a good organist," they wrote, "but certainly no math teacher."

J. S. Bach was born into a gifted musical family. He studied at his father's knee, but both of his parents died before he was ten, so he was sent to live with an older brother. By fifteen he was earning his own living as a chorister but soon took on a position as church organist. By age eighteen he was well known as a concert organist and harpsichord player. Until his last year of life, people who heard him play would note, "I never thought anyone could play like that!"

When Bach's wife of thirteen years died in 1720, Bach was a musician in the court of Prince Leopold. Within the next three years he had remarried and moved his growing family (twenty children eventually) from the secular court to Saint Thomas Church in Leipzig.

Although the town council hired him to teach Latin and math, they allowed him to be organist and chapel master. That assignment required that he compose Christian music around the church year, producing worship pieces each Sunday. He wrote 295 sacred cantatas, yet he was criticized as lacking contemporary musical insight, as being too old fashioned and too religious. Only nine or ten of his compositions were published in his lifetime. He and the town council perpetually squabbled over his contract and fulfillment of his duties, especially teaching math to boys.

When he died at age sixty-five, his library contained more books on theology and faith than on music, Latin, or mathematics. We already know how the town council eulogized him.

Bach was not fully appreciated for his gifts in his day, but we of later generations are thankful that he kept using those gifts while trying to carry on the other duties life demanded of him. Our gifts may not be at a genius level, but we still need to practice them if we are to do what God calls us to do with our lives.

—Mary C. Miller

REFLECTION

Is there a gift I'm not fully using because of demands on my schedule or because people just wouldn't understand?

PRAYER

Lord, give me the wisdom to discern my gifts and the courage to use them while life still beats within me.

"If you have a talent, use it in every which way possible. Don't hoard it. Don't dole it out like a miser. Spend it lavishly like a millionaire intent on going broke."

—Brendan Francis

152

39

STEWARDSHIP

Dad's Pencil

*Unless you are faithful in small
matters, you won't be faithful in
large ones. If you cheat even a
little, you won't be honest with
greater responsibilities. And if you
are untrustworthy about worldly
wealth, who will trust you with
the true riches of heaven? And if
you are not faithful with other
people's money, why should you be
trusted with money of your own?*

LUKE 16:10-12

SOME families tussle over whether the TV remote gets returned to its place, but perhaps the most frequent "put it back where you found it" issue in my house has been over my office supplies. It got so bad that I finally designated and stocked one drawer as the family drawer and one as mine—access forbidden.

Recently my fourth grader asked if he could borrow one of my automatic pencils because the family drawer had none. I decided it was teaching time. "Okay," I said, "but what's the rule?"

"Return it when I'm done," he responded.

An hour later he placed the pencil in the drawer and said, "Here's your pencil back, Dad."

At that moment I had a gratifying sense that my son was learning to be trustworthy. That gave me confidence to entrust things of greater value, like a Walkman tape player, to his care. My goal is to be able to entrust anything to him with the full confidence that he will treat it as I would.

Why make such a big deal about a pencil? Because learning to take care of someone else's property—stewardship—begins with small things. The issue is not the value of the item but the principle involved: faithfulness. When someone entrusts his property to you, you should take great care with it.

When we are careful to manage the small things, it shows we understand the concept. Faithful stewardship is the same whether it involves a pencil or a laptop computer. If we will compromise our faithfulness over a pencil, it shows how little we value stewardship. Why sell out your character for pennies?

That is the idea of Luke 16:10-12. Jesus teaches that how we handle the small things is one of the most important tests of character. This passage implies that one small thing God tests leaders with is money. If a leader can rightly manage God's money, that leader may be able to handle greater responsibility: the spiritual oversight of individuals and groups.

155

—Craig Brian Larson

REFLECTION

Am I managing my money as God's possession, not mine? Am I following scriptural principles of complete honesty, honoring God by donating first to his work?

PRAYER

Oh, Lord, when it comes to what you have given me, there really are no small things. Grant me grace to be a wise and faithful steward of what you have entrusted to me.

"To get money is difficult, to keep it more difficult, but to spend it wisely most difficult of all."

—Unknown

40

STRESS

The Firstborn Syndrome

You're going to wear yourself out—and the people, too. This job is too heavy a burden for you to handle all by yourself.

EXODUS 18:18

WHEN our oldest daughter was a little tyke, every night after she had gone to bed, I would march myself over to her playpen and neatly arrange all of her strewn-about toys. My wife, wiser than I was about such things, cautioned me that this was not a good idea. "First, you're already doing enough," she said. "Second, if you always do it for her, she will never learn to do it for herself."

Not taking heed to her caveat, I continued in my ways—and became increasingly bitter about having to do all of my daughter's picking up; our daughter never did learn to clean up after herself. Instead, she learned that if she didn't do it, I would. A stressed-out dad and a sloppy daughter were the only results of my meddling.

A few years ago a study reported that a disproportionate number of Christian leaders are first-born children, who, as studies have shown, are rigidly responsible. Firstborns, myself included, take great pride in being responsible and doing more than is required of them. As a result, we often overburden ourselves with responsibilities, shortchanging the people we work with by not giving them the opportunity to use their gifts.

Moses was that kind of leader, but he was fortunate enough to have a father-in-law who challenged his detrimental behavior. "Son," said Jethro, "you are not allowing the people to build a sense of responsibility."

Taking Jethro's advice to heart, Moses began to pass on some of his responsibilities to others, holding on only to those that were most central to his role as a leader. It was a good move both for Moses and for the people. The result was reduced stress, both for Moses and for the Israelites.

—Steve McKinley

REFLECTION

What burden am I carrying that I should be sharing with someone else?

PRAYER

Oh, Lord, help me loosen my grip on
_____.

"I owe whatever success I have attained, by and large, to my ability to surround myself with people who are smarter than I am."

—Andrew Carnegie, nineteenth-century industrialist

160

STRESS

The Myth of the One-Man Show

*Yet I will preserve seven thousand
others in Israel who have never
bowed to Baal or kissed him!*

1 KINGS 19:18

I WAS never a very good volleyball player, even on a full six-person team. Now I watch athletes on television effortlessly playing two-person-team beach volleyball. Although the court is much smaller than an indoor court, playing well on it would still be difficult, if not impossible, for me.

Some days I feel as if I'm a one-person volleyball team. There's more to do than I can keep up with. I run from the study to the hospital room, from the funeral home to the pulpit, and from the confirmation class to the board meeting. After a few days of this I often lapse into what is perhaps the most unlovely of all human emotions—self-pity.

The prophet Elijah also had a problem with self-pity. When Ahab and Jezebel ordered Elijah dead, he retreated to a cave, where he wallowed in his misery. When the Lord confronted him and asked him why he was sitting in the dark, Elijah lamented that it was difficult and lonely being the only person left in Israel who honored the Lord. The Lord listened and then nudged him back out into the world, reminding him that there were, in fact, still seven thousand Israelites who had not succumbed to Baal's allure. While Elijah felt isolated, he was not alone.

When I am doing my frantic run-around-and-

do-it-all-and-get-stressed-out-and-feel-sorry-for-
myself routine, I need that kind of reminder. I
mythologize my situation when I think I am the
only one who cares and works hard. I need to recognize that there are others who are ready, willing, and able to bear the heavy load of the
ministry.

Back when I did play volleyball, very often
there would be one person on the team who tried
to dominate the game by charging all over the
court, barging into people, and not letting other
team members hit their own shots. Maybe the
team would have been better if instead of
bemoaning the fact that he was stuck with such
lousy players, he had focused on doing his own
thing well and allowed others to participate.

—Steve McKinley

REFLECTION

Am I allowing other people to get in on the game, or am I trying to keep it all to myself?

PRAYER

When I'm trying to do it all, Lord, slow me down, and show me others who can help pick up the load.

"God grant me the serenity to prioritize the things I cannot delegate, the courage to say no when I need to, and the wisdom to know when to go home."

—Anonymous

164

SUFFERING

Ministry Birthed in Pain

Let us come boldly to the throne of our gracious God. There we will receive his mercy, and we will find grace to help us when we need it.

HEBREWS 4:16

I DID not have a burning-bush experience like many I know. I just grew up having faith from as far back as I can remember. But my faith was deeply shaken and challenged in my early thirties as a result of an accident and a string of losses, all in a two-year time frame.

What had appeared to be a benign accident (a fall) was the beginning of a seemingly unending nightmare for my family and me. I had been a high-energy, athletic mother of three, but suddenly I was a victim, suffering acute and apparently incurable pain. I was unable to care for my family and could not even lift my two-year-old daughter. In the midst of that my husband's forty-year-old brother died of cancer, and six weeks later my father, a doctor, died suddenly of a heart attack. For the first time in my life I questioned my faith and my reliance on God. As a child I had grown up believing that between my father and God, anything could be healed. In my grief and pain it seemed both had abandoned me.

In my darkest hour, overwhelmed with fatigue and pain, I questioned whether I wanted to go on living. Alone and weeping in my closet so my children would not see me, I cried out to God to make himself known to me, to throw me a lifeline. While I did not get a sign at that moment,

within one week I was directed to the right doc-
tors, diagnosed, and had the first of five recon-
structive surgeries on my jaws—surgeries that
would continue over the next twenty years. I was
so relieved to find an answer, and I know that
God carried me there. I had absolutely no fear
ever again that I was alone, even through years of
medical challenges. New to my church at the
time, I found the lifeline I was seeking in the
form of people, people who cared for me, and
people who cared for my husband and my children—not just once but every time there was a
need over the next twenty years. I committed my
life to ministry during my first six-month rehabil-
itation period, offering to God my gift of thanks
and promising that I, in turn, would be a lifeline
for others.

I would not have chosen my journey as a
means to growth, but I must admit that I have
grown into who I am today as a result of the
hurt—and the healing that comes through God's
grace and faithfulness.

—Sue Mallory

REFLECTION

When have I felt the grace and mercy of God in a time of great challenge or sorrow? Who has God placed in my life as that "lifeline" in times of great need?

PRAYER

Father God, thank you for your promise to walk with us through the valley and in the darkness. All I have needed your hand has provided. I know that you will never abandon me, and it is on that truth that I am able to stand during my times of sorrow.

"Reflect upon your present blessings, of which every man has plenty, not on your past misfortunes, of which all men have some."

—Charles Dickens (1812–1870), English novelist

168

43

SUFFERING

The Weeping at Birkenau

*God looks down from heaven on
the entire human race; he looks to
see if there is even one with real
understanding, one who seeks for
God.*
PSALM 53:2

IT was hot, humid, and sticky—a terrible day to be out in the blistering sun, let alone at Auschwitz, the infamous Nazi death camp.

I had been teaching English in the Czech Republic for two years and took the summer to work at an evangelistic camp there. The team of short-term missionaries and I needed some rest, so we went to Krakow, Poland. One day's agenda included a trip to Auschwitz.

I had been there the year before, horrified by the tangible presence of evil. I had no desire to return ever again. But this trip was for our leaders, Americans who needed to see firsthand some of the history deeply ingrained into the mind-set of the people they wanted to reach for Christ.

After Auschwitz we went to the massive work camp Birkenau, just a mile away. My attitude grew bitter. I wondered, *What could I possibly need to see here again?* I wandered listlessly in the heat, coming nearer to the gas chamber, unsure if I really wanted to see it. Only a few yards from the gas chamber, I stopped suddenly as I heard a sound.

As I looked up, I saw an old, graying figure of a man. He was an Orthodox Jew, a rabbi, wearing his prayer shawl and yarmulke, and his beard fell down the middle of his chest. He seemed tall, but

I could not tell for sure because he was kneeling with his face on the ground. What I had heard was his weeping—not weeping, but moaning. His body racked by emotion, he would raise and lower his arms as he cried out in Hebrew. His sobs could be heard by many of us, and small groups of tourists gathered to look at him. I looked away, embarrassed to be so close to his grief, ashamed of my pitiful expression of emotion.

Where did I have room to be angry? Before me was a man who had every right to grieve—the blood of his own people, likely his kin, had been shed on this spot. A new sense of loss came over me as I thought about how deep his suffering must be—a pain still fresh after fifty years.

171

Suddenly, I had a picture of God's heart for his Son. For the first time I saw Birkenau not as a memorial to the evil acts of humanity but to the massive, terrible price God paid through the loss of his Son. I needed to hear the grief of Birkenau to remember my Father's cost when he let go of his only child.

—Linda Gehrs

REFLECTION

How aware am I of the suffering of Christians around the world today? What is my obligation toward these persecuted brothers and sisters?

PRAYER

Lord, have mercy on me.

"The world and the Cross do not get along too well together, and comfort and holiness do not share the same room."

—Carlo Carretto (1910–1988), spiritual writer

44

TEMPTATION

Can You Spot the Lie?

*My son, pay attention to my
wisdom, listen well to my words of
insight, that you may maintain
discretion and your lips may
preserve knowledge. For the lips of
an adulteress drip honey, and her
speech is smoother than oil; but in
the end she is bitter as gall, sharp
as a double-edged sword.*
PROVERBS 5:1-4, NIV

OCCASIONALLY I ask my children to "spot the lie" when we're watching a TV commercial. A sleek red sports car will get you a tall brunette. Lie! The right microbrew will deliver happiness and companionship. Lie! Wearing the right brand of clothes will give you an edge over your competition. Lie! Television commercials often skew reality in their attempt to lure us into buying a product. They promise more than they can deliver. And all the news in commercials is good—no mention of the harm some products can inflict (those alluring microbrews, for example).

Temptation operates the same way. It comes wrapped in an attractive package. Satan is too smart to approach us and say, "Excuse me, could I have an hour of your time so I can ruin your life?" If he did, temptation would be easy to flee. But temptation is subtle. As the sage in Proverbs 5 points out, the appeal of an adulteress resembles honey and oil—the sweetest substances known in the ancient Near East. But in truth the adulteress's appeal is more like gall and a sword. Gall was the most bitter substance known in that region, while a sword represented grave danger.

According to Proverbs, gaining the wisdom and insight that leads to discretion is important. A person with discretion has a streetwise knowledge of the dark side. She understands the information that temptation's sales pitch conveniently omits. He is aware of the alleys temptation will take us down—if we let it.

Joe Aldrich, former president of Multnomah Bible College, warns, "When you're tempted to sin, especially in the area of sexuality, think through the logical consequences of sin which are tempting you. Don't stop your fantasy with the act. Think about the next morning, the next month, and the next year of your life. What will happen to your family, your children, your ministry?"

Sometimes we assume that we'll outgrow our vulnerability to temptation or that our Christian maturity or life experience will protect us. But leaders are not exempt from temptation; if anything, we may face more intense temptations than others do. After all, the stakes are higher. Satan has more to gain from a leader's downfall.

Satan knows too well each of our particular areas of vulnerability, and he will exploit them however he can. Temptation lurks behind our desires and weaknesses, ready to make its inviting appeal. And when it does, it never tells us, as commentator Paul Harvey would say, the rest of the story.

—Steve Mathewson

REFLECTION

What temptation looks especially attractive to me?
What might the logical consequences be if I gave in
to this temptation?

PRAYER

Lord, you know how I struggle with _____. You
know how I long for _____. So armor me that the
enemy can't penetrate these weaknesses. Grant me
the discernment to recognize temptation for what
it is. And when I am tempted, help me to find a
way out—as you promise in your Word.

"The devil's most devilish when respectable."

—Elizabeth Barrett Browning,
nineteenth-century English poet

176

TEMPTATION

Lion at the Door

Sin is waiting to attack and destroy you, and you must subdue it.

GENESIS 4:7

EVERY leader has a weakness, maybe several.
Weaknesses are doorways to the dangers that
lurk nearby, waiting to catch us in a careless
moment. Wise leaders know that their position
and accomplishments, rather than insulate them
from temptation, may actually make them bigger
targets. More responsibilities mean more doors to
guard. Outside each door crouch temptations
waiting to pounce.

It's not just the surprise attack that devours
leaders, however. Often temptation comes subtly,
disguised as something innocent and good.
Temptations can come hidden beneath noble
deeds. What seems to be a cuddly lamb may in
fact be a hungry lion.

Cain began with seemingly benign intentions
to worship God. He brought an offering—crops
raised with his own hands. Unfortunately, Cain's
worthy ambitions fell short of God's expectations.
We can't be sure exactly how his offering was
deficient. All we know is that Cain did not give
his offering in faith, as Abel did (Heb. 11:4).

Even after Cain's flawed attempt at worship,
he was not ruined. Cain had an opportunity to
make things right, even after jealousy and competition enraged him and turned his brother into a
rival. God warned Cain, urging him to make the

right choice. He unmasked the temptation that was lurking near Cain and revealed its true nature. Sin was out to consume Cain's life, God told him, but Cain could still conquer the temptation if he wanted.

Cain's story offers hope for leaders grappling with their humanity. When sin crouches outside our door, or when we fall short of God's expectations, God still gives us the opportunity to regain control of the situation. Through his grace, God offers us another chance. God wants to empower us to face temptation and overcome it. It's our choice.

Cain's problem is ours. Our human nature gets in the way. No matter how determined we may be, no matter how willing our spirits may be, our flesh remains weak (Matt. 26:41). This is not reason to surrender, however. Temptation need not devour us just because we're weak. Instead, we can look to God's grace to compensate for our weakness: "My grace is sufficient for you," God told one tormented by Satan, "for my power is made perfect in weakness" (2 Cor. 12:9, NIV).

Temptation stalks everyone, including those who lead God's people. But with God's help, we can master it.

—Richard Doebler

179

REFLECTION

What makes me most susceptible to temptation—my unguarded overconfidence or the temptation's deceptive nature?

PRAYER

Lord, help me keep my eyes wide open—not merely to the deceptive schemes of the enemy but also to the weaknesses and limitations of my own flesh.

"My temptations have been my masters in divinity."

—Martin Luther (1483–1546),
German Reformation leader

TIME MANAGEMENT

Wanted: A Few Unbusy Leaders

*God blessed the seventh day and
declared it holy, because it was the
day when he rested from his work
of creation.*
GENESIS 2:3

ONE of the restaurants my wife and I frequent has a section on its menu called "Guilt-Free Desserts," which is designed to appeal to all of us who worry about our weight and cholesterol. It is a delight to think that there is a dessert you can eat and enjoy without feeling guilty.

But I've never heard of anything called guilt-free resting. If anything, busyness is increasingly becoming a badge of honor, and Christian leaders are among the best at claiming that badge of honor. Imagine a scenario of four Christian leaders trying to establish a time to meet. Three of them whip out Day-Timers and electronic organizers, shake their heads, and confess that the best time to meet would be in about seventeen months.

Then the fourth person says, "Schedule it anytime. I'm not real busy"—and the other three stare in amazement. "Not real busy?" they echo incredulously, believing that all Christian leaders who serve devoutly take pride in their busyness.

Yet I think the world could use some unbusy Christian leaders who would testify to the truth that the world is in God's hands, not our own. Nothing is wrong with hard work—with pouring ourselves wholeheartedly into what we are doing in the service of the gospel of Jesus Christ, but we need to rest. Even God rested, and the Old Testament is forthright about keeping the Sabbath as a day of rest. As Christian leaders we have the responsibility of building time into our own schedules to rest and be refreshed. If God could look back at six days of creative work and call it good, then maybe we as Christian leaders should do the same.

—Steve McKinley

REFLECTION

Am I keeping the Sabbath by planning a time in my schedule for adequate rest?

PRAYER

Lord of the Sabbath, help me to make rest and refreshment a priority, and free me from the need to be indispensable.

"I am not the Christ."

—John the Baptist

184

TIME MANAGEMENT

Diversions and Distractions

*Make the most of every
opportunity for doing good in
these evil days.*

EPHESIANS 5:16

IT was one of those defining moments—a moment of enlightenment.

I was eighteen and wanted to entertain my five-year-old brother, so I offered to take him to the rides at the county fair. With twenty-one dollars in my pocket, I was the model big brother.

Through the gate into the fairgrounds we went, past the farm implements, the livestock barns, the hot dog and popcorn stands, the craft buildings with jams and quilts. We had one thing on our minds: the rides. The towering Ferris wheel marked our destination.

Unfortunately, we didn't make it. A distraction diverted us. Just past the gaming area I heard a hawker call my name. Or so I thought. I spun around to see who was calling, and a man in a booth beckoned me over.

Suffice it to say that within five minutes he had most of my money, and I was still five points away from winning the stuffed panda.

That's when I came to my senses. I was angry at the hawker, but mostly I was angry with myself. I'd lost seventeen dollars and several rides for my brother. But I learned a lesson: Distractions can sidetrack you from your goal.

The Bible tells us to live wisely by making the most of our opportunities and by understanding

God's will (Eph. 5:15-17). Three time-management principles emerge from these verses:

1. Know your destination. Discover God's will and purpose, and you'll use your time more effectively. If God wants us in Dallas, we're wasting our time traveling to the Grand Canyon or the rocky faces of Mount Rushmore.

2. Make the most of every opportunity. We can create opportunities when we have to, but if we're ready for them when they come, we save time. Bear Bryant, Alabama's famous football coach, told of his early days at Kentucky. His team fumbled the ball in front of the bench, and in the resulting scramble someone kicked over a box containing eight more footballs. A free-for-all ensued, with Tennessee recovering five balls and Kentucky four. The officials gave possession to Tennessee. The moral: When the ball comes bouncing your way, grab it. Seize every opportunity that comes along.

3. Be careful how you live. Wiser now, I'm not distracted by hawkers at the fair. But urgent needs still try to distract me from my main purpose and vision. When we manage our time effectively, we will work at not allowing the urgent to keep us from what is most important.

—Richard Doebler

REFLECTION

Can I tell the difference between a distraction that could detour me from God's purpose and an unexpected opportunity that should be seized?

PRAYER

Since you've called me and given me resources to answer your call, Lord, help me use wisely the time you've given me and not abuse it.

"Hurry, then, is not just a disordered schedule. Hurry is a disordered heart."

—John Ortberg, pastor and writer

48

TIME MANAGEMENT

What You and Bill Gates Have in Common

There is a time for everything, a season for every activity under heaven.

ECCLESIASTES 3:1

WHILE I ate my lunch at my desk, I was surfing the Net and came across a Web page that tracks the wealth of Microsoft founder Bill Gates. As I stared in amazement at the figures on the screen, the receptionist called me out to talk with Mark, a local street person who sometimes stops by and asks for a few dollars. From Mark's perspective, I'm sure that my wealth, even in comparison to Bill Gates's wealth, is astonishing.

Distribution of wealth is unequal, but time is absolutely equitable. Bill Gates, Mark, you, and I may not be equally wealthy, but we all have 168 hours every week. Yet all of us must decide how we are going to spend those 168 hours. Like the way I spend my money, the way I spend my time should be a reflection of my priorities. If it isn't, something is wrong.

In his book *The 7 Habits of Highly Effective People*, Stephen Covey points out that the "urgent" has a way of overwhelming the "important." We get so tied up doing things that we think need to be done immediately that we don't have time to do the things that would truly build the church eternally. When the property committee comes charging through the church office door enraged, battling over the proper colors to be used in the men's restroom, we find ourselves putting aside planning our outreach mission to the community. The urgent has won out over the important, and we've squandered a portion of the week's 168 hours.

It's inevitable that we will sometimes waste part of our 168 hours. But if the urgent squeezes out the important regularly, we've got a problem.

—Steve McKinley

REFLECTION

What would have to change in my life for the
important to take precedence over the urgent?

PRAYER

Lord, you created time and gave it to us as a gift.
Help us to use it to your glory and honor.

"All my possessions for a moment of time."

—Queen Elizabeth I, as she died

49

⌒ VISION

Fulfilling God's Dream

> As he slept, he dreamed of a
> stairway that reached from earth
> to heaven. And he saw the angels
> of God going up and down on it.
>
> At the top of the stairway stood
> the Lord, and he said, "I am the
> Lord, the God of your grandfather
> Abraham and the God of your
> father, Isaac. The ground you are
> lying on belongs to you. I will give
> it to you and your descendants."
>
> GENESIS 28:12-13

THE high school commencement speaker was giving a rather conventional address. "It is important for you, as you go forth," he said, "to have a great dream. Dream big things, great things."

The speaker didn't quote any Scripture, but I immediately thought of Jacob's dream the night he was on the run from his angry brother. A great ladder was let down from heaven, with angels ascending and descending on it. In that dream Jacob got a new vision for his life. He saw that his life was meant to count for something, that he ought to go back, make peace with his brother, and live a better life.

Then I caught myself and realized that this was not exactly what the story implied. There were angels ascending, taking messages from earth up to the throne of God, but there were also angels descending. Angels were busy bringing messages down from heaven to earth.

Christians are those who believe in large, ambitious dreams. But our dreams are not exclusively self-derived. It is important for us to have a dream, some vision for what our lives ought to be. But we ought not to forget that in our dreaming, God is also dreaming. The story of Jacob's ladder implies not only that we have dreams of God but that God has dreams for us.

One of the great joys of Christian leadership is to be part of something larger than one's self. We are busy living out a career, but the word *career* doesn't do justice to the demands or the benefits of Christian service. One of the things that makes Christian leadership a great way to spend our lives is that we are busy living out the dreams of God. You are God's ambassador, God's instrument. You are an aspect of God's dream for the future. There is business, conversation, communication between heaven and earth, and your life is part of it.

A man in my church who was in construction was commissioned to build a massive bridge over the Mississippi River. This required him to be away from his family and friends. He also had to work long hours six days a week.

But when he returned, he told me what a great joy his six months working on that bridge had been.

"A joy?" I asked.

"Yes, a joy," he said. "Pastor, it is a rare and great thing to have your life used for something bigger than you."

We leaders ought to be reminded frequently of what a joy it is to have our little lives caught up in something bigger than ourselves.

—William Willimon

REFLECTION

Am I often tempted to lose sight of the larger picture God creates and keep narrowly focused on the daily nuts and bolts?

PRAYER

God, help me to remember that life isn't just about projects and meetings and cranky computers, but that in you I'm part of a much greater purpose.

"It is a fundamental principle in the life and walk of faith that we must always be prepared for the unexpected when we are dealing with God."

—D. Martyn Lloyd-Jones, twentieth-century pastor and author

50

WORDS

Getting the Garbage Out

*People can tame all kinds of
animals and birds and reptiles
and fish, but no one can tame the
tongue. It is an uncontrollable
evil, full of deadly poison.*
JAMES 3:7-8

IT was late on a June afternoon when we pulled off Interstate 94 into a rest area in eastern Montana. Erin, my three-year-old daughter, needed to use the rest room. My mother, Erin's grandma, took Erin by the hand and walked up the paved path toward the facilities. As they neared the rest room, my mom felt a tug as Erin bent down to look at a young rattlesnake coiled on the path. Young rattlers have not yet learned to measure the venom they inject, so their bites can be lethal. Fortunately, this snake slithered away instead of striking Erin.

Many potentially dangerous animals roam the Western wilderness—rattlesnakes, mountain lions, grizzly bears. But the most deadly creature of all is closer than you think. It's a creature, says James, that none of us can tame: the tongue. The tongue's deadly poison can shatter self-esteem, crush a joyful spirit, trigger anger, and divide friends. The tongue is a contradiction. The same tongue that sang "Praise God from Whom All Blessings Flow" in worship can, thirty minutes later, suddenly lash out at a spouse or a child on the drive home from church.

If no one can tame this dangerous animal, what can we do? Throughout Scripture we're advised to think before we speak, and many of us have learned from hard experience not to blurt out the first words that come to mind. Yet the ultimate solution runs deeper: Tame not only the tongue but the thoughts that motivate the tongue. Envy, bitterness, unresolved resentments, pride, selfishness, impulsiveness—all lie behind our unbridled speech. We need to clean the garbage out of our hearts, admitting our weaknesses to God and asking him to deal with our sinfulness. Then our tongues will settle down, tamed and harmless.

—Steve Mathewson

REFLECTION

When was the last time I said something I regretted? What was behind it? How have I tried to control these tendencies?

PRAYER

God, give me discernment to know when to speak and when not to. Help me to curb the impulse to say the first thing that comes to mind. Help me to listen more and speak less. Most of all, though, clean the garbage out of my heart—and fill those spaces with what is pure and godly and positive and true. Fill those spaces with your Spirit!

"Words are as beautiful as wild horses and sometimes as difficult to corral."

—Ted Berkman, biographer and screenwriter

200

51

WORK

It's Not My Job

*My job was to plant the seed in
your hearts, and Apollos watered
it, but it was God, not we, who
made it grow.*

1 CORINTHIANS 3:6

WHEN I began to plant the church I now lead in Cincinnati, I expended tremendous amounts of energy to get it off the ground. I spoke with some fifteen hundred people over a two-year period, sharing my vision for this new church and mustering up as much enthusiasm as I could. Yet in spite of all of this effort, our first Sunday service saw only thirty-seven in attendance. A little bit of math shows that's a rejection rate of over 97 percent! It was then that I rediscovered the verse above: It is our job to do the planting and watering but God's to make growth happen.

I have come to realize that I spent the first part of my Christian life exerting a tremendous amount of human effort trying to accomplish what only God can do: to bring about a harvest of fruit. Yes, I am called to be diligent about planting and watering, but I am not responsible for the final result.

This insight has encouraged me as a leader and has reminded me of my limitations. I can become anxious about ministry ventures, wondering if something I've invested a lot of effort in will ever come to fruition. It is then that I have to sit back and pray, "Well, God, I've done about all I can do. I guess now you've got a challenge. I've

planted and watered, and I will keep on watering
the best I know how, but you are the one who has
to bring about a harvest."

I no longer believe I can do a big thing. As a
leader, all I am really capable of doing are the
small things. But a small thing done consistently
in the hands of God is capable of changing the
world. God is looking for leaders who are willing
to do small things, who are willing to be diligent,
and then who are willing to get out of the way.

—Steve Sjogren

REFLECTION

Can I be content with doing that small thing for God, or do I have a need to do the big, splashy, visible thing?

PRAYER

God, you know how long I've been trying to make _____ happen. Sometimes I get so discouraged and feel my efforts are getting nowhere. Work within me so that I can turn the results of this over to you and feel content that I've done what I can on your behalf.

"We are too little to be able always to rise above difficulties. Well, then, let us pass beneath them quite simply."

— Thérèse of Lisieux, twentieth-century mystic

204

52

WORK

The Value of Mistakes

*An empty stable stays clean, but
no income comes from an empty
stable.*

PROVERBS 14:4

HOWARD Head was frustrated with the clumsy, hickory snow skis he used when he hit the slopes. So he designed new skis with two layers of aluminum, plywood sidewalls, and a center filled with honeycombed plastic. He excitedly tried them out on the slopes, but they broke. So he made a second pair. They broke, too—as did the third pair. Howard Head went through forty versions of skis over three years. Finally, in 1950 he came up with a design that worked, and his sporting equipment is known worldwide today.

Leaders who expect progress must allow some latitude for chaos and failure. That's the point of Proverbs 14:4. Derek Kidner, an Old Testament scholar, comments, "Orderliness can reach the point of sterility. This proverb is not a plea for slovenliness, physical or moral, but for the readiness to accept upheaval, and a mess to clear up as the price of growth." Do you want your feeding trough kept clean? Fine, then don't have any oxen. But you'll have a tough time harvesting and processing your grain.

Peter Drucker recognizes this wisdom when it comes to business. He suggests, "The better a man is, the more mistakes he will make, for the more new things he will try. I would never promote into a top-level job a man who was not making mistakes—otherwise he is sure to be mediocre." Another CEO adds, "Make sure you generate a reasonable number of mistakes."

Churches and ministries that make an impact create an environment where people are allowed to make mistakes. Obsession with complete order will curb creativity. Do you want the walls in your church facility to be spotless, or do you want to reach more teens for Jesus Christ? Is it more important to avoid legal hassles and red tape or to develop a ministry to single moms? Leaders must create environments for themselves and others that allow for a reasonable amount of mess. That's the price for progress.

—Steve Mathewson

REFLECTION

What kinds of messes and mistakes can I allow people to make in order to make progress? What kinds of messes and mistakes are inappropriate because they stem from carelessness, rebellion, or apathy?

PRAYER

Lord, save me from majoring on the minors. Help me to see the big picture—and to tolerate the messiness that comes with effective and creative ministry.

"You may be disappointed if you fail, but you are doomed if you don't try!"

—Beverly Sills, American soprano

⮎CONTRIBUTORS

David Goetz, compiler, contributor, and general editor, is founder of CustomZines.com, an internet publishing services company based in Wheaton, Illinois. He is former manager of new product development for Christianity Today International and served as associate editor of *Leadership* journal and executive editor of PreachingToday.com. He and his wife, Jana, live in Wheaton with their three children.

⮎

OTHER CONTRIBUTORS
Peter Barnes is senior pastor of First Presbyterian Church in Boulder, Colorado.

James D. Berkley is senior associate pastor of First Presbyterian Church in Bellevue, Washington. He is a contributing editor to *Leadership* journal and the author of *The Dynamics of Church Finance.*

Paul Borden is a consultant for American Baptist Churches of the West in Oakland, California, and also consults internationally, advising churches in Australia and New Zealand. He is a contributor to the *Building Church Leaders Notebook,* PreachingToday.com, and Preaching Today Audio and was also the biblical and theological editor for two compact discs, *Old Testament* and *New Testament Foundations with Philip Yancey.*

Jill Briscoe is director of Telling the Truth media ministry and editor of *Just Between Us,* a magazine for ministry wives and women in ministry. A popular conference speaker, she is the author of more than forty books and coauthor with Kay Arthur and Carole Mayhall of *Can a Busy Christian Develop Her Spiritual Life? Answers to Questions Women Ask About Spirituality.*

Bob Buford is founder of Leadership Network, an organization that supports innovation and excellence in churches. He is author of *Half-Time: Changing Your Game Plan from Success to Significance.* For many years he was chairman of the board and CEO of Buford Television, Inc., a Texas-based cable TV company.

Max De Pree is chairman of the board at Herman Miller, Inc. He has been named by *Fortune* to the National Business Hall of Fame and is the author of *Leadership Is an Art* and *Leadership Jazz.*

Richard Doebler is senior pastor of Cloquet Gospel Tabernacle in Cloquet, Minnesota, and a contributing editor to *Leadership* journal. In addition, he served as an editor for *The Quest Study Bible* as well as *Your Church* and *Computing Today* magazines.

Gary Fenton is senior pastor of Dawson Baptist Church in Birmingham, Alabama. A speaker on the subject of leadership and motivation, he is the author of *Your Ministry's Next Chapter* and coauthor of *Mastering Church Finances.*

Mark Galli is editor of *Christian History* magazine and managing editor of *Christianity Today* magazine. He also served as a Presbyterian pastor for ten years in Mexico City and in Sacramento, California. He is coauthor of *Preaching That Connects* and *The Complete Idiot's Guide to Prayer.*

Linda Gehrs is assistant editor for *Men of Integrity,* a men's devotional; *Preaching Today,* a sermon audio series; and *Building Church Leaders Notebook*. Before working for Christianity Today International, she taught English as a foreign language for two years in the Czech Republic and volunteered for six months with Josiah Venture, a mission focusing on youth ministry and leadership development in Eastern Europe.

Carl F. George is a church consultant, the author of *Prepare Your Church for the Future* and coauthor of *The Coming Church Revolution* and *Leading and Managing Your Church*.

David Goetz is founder of CustomZines.com and formerly executive editor of PreachingToday.com. He was also general editor for *Building Church Leaders Notebook* and the Pastor's Soul Series.

Mark Hatfield, now retired, is longtime U.S. senator from Oregon.

Harry J. Heintz is senior pastor of Brunswick Presbyterian Church in Troy, New York, and mentor at Gordon-Conwell Theological Seminary.

Craig Brian Larson is pastor of Lake Shore Church in Chicago, Illinois, and editor of PreachingToday.com and Preaching Today Audio. He is coauthor of *Preaching That Connects*.

Sue Mallory is the executive director of Leadership Training Network, an organization designed to equip and mobilize church leadership, and supporting author of the *Starter Kit for Mobilizing Ministry*. She also founded and was the first president of the Southern California Association for Lay Empowerment and Development.

Steve Mathewson is senior pastor of Dry Creek Bible Church in Belgrade, Montana. He is a contributor to

The Quest Study Bible and *Building Church Leaders Notebook*. Steve's sermons have been featured on the Preaching Today audio series.

John Maxwell is founder and president of INJOY, Inc., an institute for developing leaders. Previously he was pastor at Skyline Wesleyan Church in Lemon Grove, California. He is the author of *Developing the Leader Within You, Developing the Leaders Around You,* and *The 21 Irrefutable Laws of Leadership.*

Steve McKinley is senior pastor of House of Prayer Lutheran Church in Richfield, Minnesota. He is a magazine columnist, a contributor to several books, and the author of *The Parboiled Pastor.*

Kevin A. Miller is vice president of resources for Christianity Today International and editor-at-large of *Leadership* journal. Kevin is the author of *Secrets of Staying Power* and coauthor with his wife, Karen, of *More Than You and Me.*

Mary C. Miller is corporate secretary of the Evangelical Covenant Church. Previously she was pastor of Donaldson Evangelical Covenant Church in Donaldson, Indiana. She is also a contributor to *Leadership* journal.

Mark Mittelberg is executive vice president of the Willow Creek Association and coauthor of *Becoming a Contagious Christian,* a book and training course.

Earl Palmer is pastor of University Presbyterian Church in Seattle, Washington. He has written a number of books and commentaries, including *Signposts: Christian Values in an Age of Uncertainty* and *Mastering Teaching.*

Ben Patterson is dean of the chapel at Hope College in Holland, Michigan. He previously served Presbyterian

(PCUSA) pastorates in New Jersey and California. He is the author of *Waiting: Find Hope When God Seems Silent*, a back-page columnist for *Leadership* journal, and a contributor to *Christianity Today*.

Ed Rowell is teaching pastor at The People's Church in Franklin, Tennessee. Previously he was associate editor of *Leadership* journal and editor of *Preaching Today* and has also served two churches in Arizona.

Steve Sjogren is senior pastor of Vineyard Community Church in Cincinnati, Ohio, which is an outreach church with weekend attendance of more than four thousand. A pioneer of servant evangelism, an innovative approach to sharing Christ, he is also the author of *Conspiracy of Kindness* and *Servant Warfare*.

Joni Eareckson Tada is founder of JAF Ministries, a parachurch organization in Agoura Hills, California, that advocates the cause of and ministers to those with disabilities. She is the author of *Heaven* and *More Precious than Silver: 366 Daily Devotional Readings*.

Rich Tatum is Web project supervisor for Christianity Today International in Carol Stream, Illinois. He was the online project supervisor for the launch of PreachingToday.com.

William Willimon has been dean of the chapel and professor of Christian Ministry at Duke University in Durham, North Carolina, since 1984 and preaches each Sunday in the Duke Chapel. He is the author of forty-three books, including *Sighing for Eden* and *What's Right with the Church*.

Randal C. Working is associate pastor for adult ministries at the First Presbyterian Church of Bellevue, Washington. For several years he worked as a campus minister with Youth for Christ in Switzerland and as an associate pastor in California.

Zig Ziglar is a motivational speaker and author of *See You at the Top*, *Over the Top*, and *Confessions of a Grieving Christian*.

214

⇒INDEX OF TOPICS

Bold entries indicate the topic under which the devotion appears in the book. Other entries are related topics that the devotion also addresses.

INDEX OF
SCRIPTURE REFERENCES

⟜ APPENDIX

The following is a list of sources in which previously published devotionals appeared.

"No Easy Work" by Max De Pree is based on material previously published in *Leadership* journal under the title "Visionary Jazz," summer 1994, by Christianity Today International.

"United in Suffering" by David Goetz is based on material previously published in the Church Leaders Online newsletter under the title "Community for the Comfortable: Some Growth Comes Only through Suffering," November 17, 1999, by Christianity Online.

"The Lie of Loneliness" by Ben Patterson was taken from *Deepening Your Conversation with God*, published in 1999 by Bethany House Publishers.

"Better Than Optimism" by Zig Ziglar is based on material previously published in *Leadership* journal under the title "More Oxygen to the Flame," fall 1998, by Christianity Today International.

"Questions for Better Decisions" by Carl F. George is based on material previously published in *Leadership* journal under the title "Beyond the Firehouse Syndrome," winter 1985, by Christianity Today International.

"Not off the Hook" by Mark Mittelberg is based on material previously published in *Leadership* journal under the title "Evangelism That Flows," summer 1998, by Christianity Today International.

"Ordering Priorities" by Mark O. Hatfield is based on material previously published in *Leadership* journal under the title "Integrity under Pressure," spring 1988, by Christianity Today International.

"A Heart for Others" by John Maxwell is based on material previously published in *Leadership* journal under the title "The Potential Around You," fall 1996, by Christianity Today International.

"Inconvenient Opportunity" by Jill Briscoe is based on material previously published in *Leadership* journal under the title "Keeping the Adventure in Your Ministry," summer 1996, by Christianity Today International.

"No Empty Time" by Joni Eareckson Tada is based on material previously published in *Leadership* journal under the title "Thriving with Limitations," winter 1996, by Christianity Today International.

"The Weeping at Birkenau" by Linda Gehrs is based on material previously published in the Church Leaders Online newsletter under the title "The Price of Letting Go: What God Lost When He Sent His Son," February 24, 1999, by Christianity Online.

LEADERSHIP RESOURCES FROM TYNDALE HOUSE PUBLISHERS, INC.

Jesus on Leadership by C. Gene Wilkes: Seven principles of leadership based on Christ's example

Leadership Prayers by Richard Kriegbaum: Prayers and reflections on being an effective leader

Leadership Devotions compiled by David Goetz: Fifty-two devotions focusing on building the internal character of Christian leaders

Leadership Meditations compiled by David Goetz: Fifty-two meditations focusing on the external aspects of leadership

ADDITIONAL MATERIALS FROM LEADERSHIP RESOURCES

Preaching Today Online
This Web site offers paid subscribers access to weekly illustrations for preaching, practical journal articles, and a searchable database for illustrations and quotations. For more information, visit www.preachingtoday.com.

Preaching Today Audio
Subscribers receive monthly two sermons and one workshop on preaching from teachers such as Bill Hybels and Haddon Robinson as well as printed sermon transcripts. To subscribe, call 1-800-806-7796.

Building Church Leaders Notebook
Provides twelve timely themes from which pastors can train their church leaders. Each chapter includes an interview with a respected church leader, practical assessment tools, case studies, and devotionals. To order, call 1-800-806-7798.

Building Church Leaders Quarterly
Provides subscribers with training materials for those in church leadership. New themes begin every three months. Included with each theme is a softcover book containing interviews, performance assessments, case studies, devotionals, and other activities. To subscribe, call 1-800-806-7796.

Leadership Resources is a division of Christianity Today International.

Leadership®